PERFORMATIVE SKYSCRAPER
TALL BUILDING DESIGN NOW

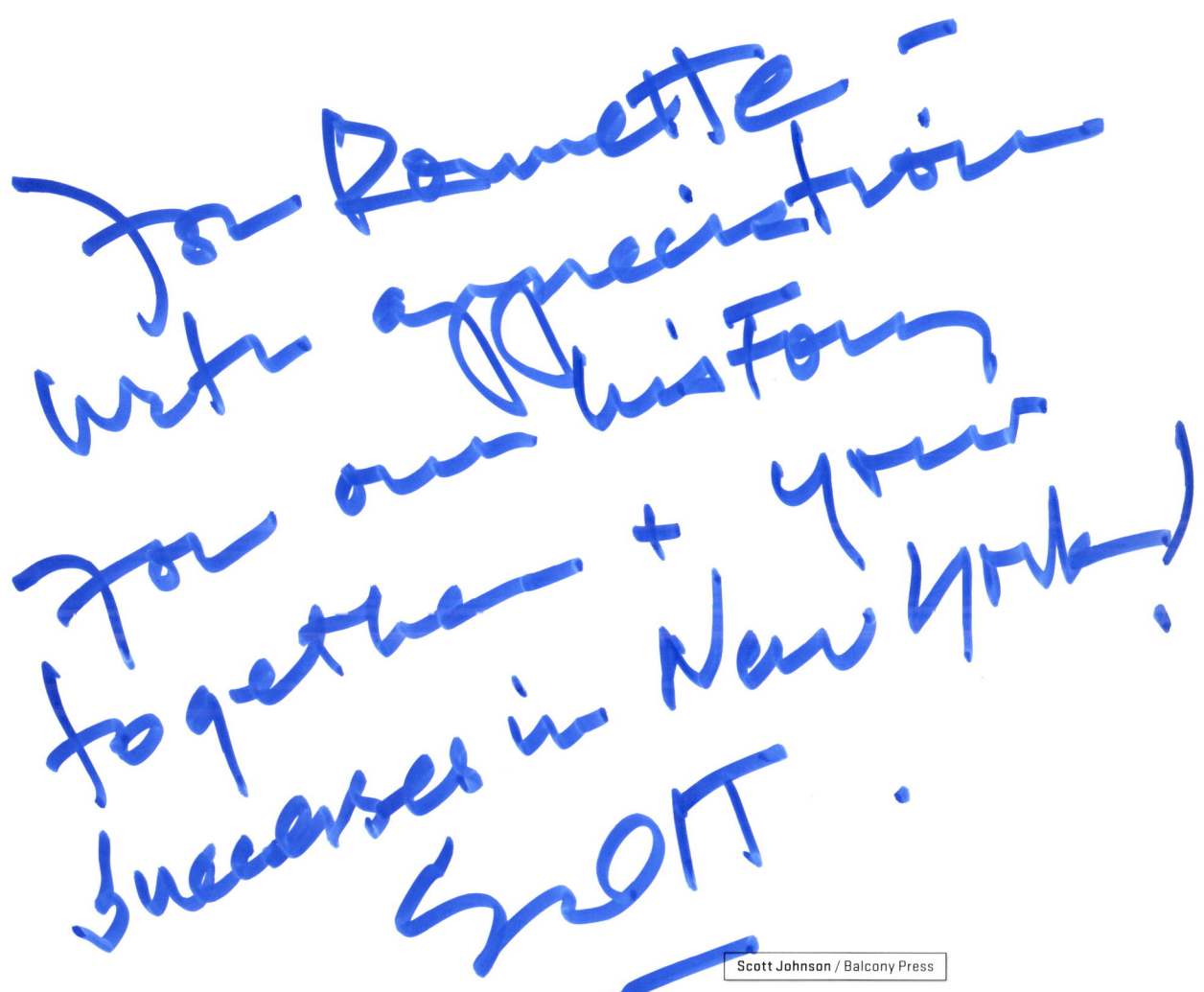

First Edition © 2014 Scott Johnson

No part of this book may be reproduced
in any manner without written permission
except in the case of brief quotations
embodied in critical articles and reviews.

Published in the United States of America
in 2014 by Balcony Press.

For information address Balcony Media, Inc.
512 E. Wilson Avenue, Suite 213, Glendale
California 91206.

Design by DISTINC
Printing and production by
Navigator Cross-Media
Printed in South Korea

Library of Congress
Control Number: 20139551547
ISBN 978-1-890449-66-7

"ACTUALLY, I DIDN'T MAKE THAT DECISION.
MY MACHINE MADE THAT DECISION."

Franklyn Berry, engineer for a Ned Kahn sculpture in Playa Vista, California, in response to a question by the architects.

PG_4_PERFORMATIVE_SKYSCRAPER.

CONTENTS

AUTHOR'S_NOTE_PG_7

PREFACE_JOSEPH_GIOVANNINI_PG_9

INTRODUCTION_PG_23

CHAPTER-ONE_PERFORMATIVE_ECOLOGIES_PG_26

CHAPTER-TWO_PERFORMATIVE_SKINS_PG_58

CHAPTER-THREE_PERFORMATIVE_PARAMETRICS_PG_80

CHAPTER-FOUR_PERFORMATIVE_NEIGHBORHOODS_PG_104

CHAPTER-FIVE_PERFORMATIVE_CITIES_PG_126

BIBILOGRAPHY_PG_156

PHOTOGRAPHY_CREDITS_PG_162

ACKNOWLEDGEMENTS_PG_164

PG_6_PERFORMATIVE_SKYSCRAPER.

AUTHOR'S NOTE

One of my most compelling classes at Harvard years ago was with William LeMessurier, the noted structural engineer who designed some of America's best known tall buildings. While we did not discuss architectural design per se, his pedagogical approach to explaining the structural design of his own buildings was intellectual, exploratory and flexible. His usual pattern was to pace in front of the chalkboard, stopping frequently to exchange cigarette and chalk between his two hands in order to diagram a yet additional and different way to analyze the same building he had just been discussing. In the end, he seemed to be searching intuitively for both the most comprehensive and efficient way to think about the structure of a tall building. Notwithstanding the intermingled smoke and chalk dust which hung in the room, there was a kind of elegance to his central act. From this, and events which followed, we learned that there are multiple vantages from which to consider the same phenomenon, in this case, tall buildings. While Bill did the work mostly in his head and on the chalkboard, the design profession years later, armed with performative criteria and high-powered tools, is still looking for a comprehensive and efficient approach to the design of tall buildings.

Following the university years, I had the pleasure of apprenticing with a number of architects well-trained in the design of tall buildings, the last of which was Philip Johnson. In that period, while many things were important to us in design, I cannot say comprehensiveness and efficiency were at the top of our list. Suffice it to say that, as design architects for any given project, we acted as the leader of a large team of consultants, most of whom we had selected. We generally made conceptual drawings of the buildings with their limited consultation, after which, the drawings were sent around for review by the team. The direction of the design was set and engineering and more specialized studies would then commence. Another architectural firm generally produced the construction documents and as the work progressed, we reviewed and commented on the final outcomes. Since then, tall buildings have changed, our expectations of their performance levels and our ability to measure them have changed, the tools with which we design them have changed, and the interdependence of architecture and engineering has changed.

The impetus behind this book is the degree of change we have experienced in the design of tall buildings in the profession at large, and at Johnson Fain in particular, over the past two decades. Additionally, for me and members of my staff, there have been university design studios, seminars and symposia as well as books and more than a few articles written during that time. Oddly, perhaps the signal event which encouraged us to feel that we might have some authority on this topic was the considerable research we did surrounding an unfortunate dispute between the overseers of the Nasher Sculpture Center and our clients at Museum Tower in Dallas. Over the course of almost two years, we and a wide-ranging team of technical consultants researched projects worldwide in search of potential solutions for glass reflection from our building into the Center's skylights which had been oriented in the direction of our building. This research took us deep into the various realms of glass technologies, shading strategies, energy effects, wind testing, structural engineering, nanotechnology, coatings, films, tints and yes, bird habitats.

All of this suggested to me that we should record some of our findings in a broader context. We have done that and since this is, in many cases, the record of other people's work, I would like to thank the many brilliant people along the way who contributed to our current understanding of tall buildings. These chapters are dedicated to young architects and enthusiastic observers of the skyscraper everywhere who want to know what's new and who stand to benefit from these many contributions.

PG_8_PERFORMATIVE_SKYSCRAPER.

PREFACE

JOSEPH_GIOVANNINI

With "Performative Skyscraper: Tall Building Design Now," Los Angeles-based architect and author Scott Johnson ventures straight into the thick of current architecture discourse, quietly producing a manifesto that points a way through a field currently splitting into mitotic delirium: architecture has become a free-for-all of pluralistic forms and approaches proliferating without any coherent theory. Computers, adding to the rampant pluralism, have been used widely in architecture for more than three decades, but especially over the last ten years they have superseded their function as obedient drafting tools to become active, increasingly independent agents of both optimization and generative design, dislocating architects from their traditional roles as the omniscience behind a building. "The computer did it," quotes Johnson, citing an anonymous architect standing proudly on a dispassionate stratum of data rather than floating adrift on a sea of aesthetic whim and theoretical speculation. Data are the firm new ground.

The book is a retroactive manifesto describing a computer-driven, performance-based approach to the design of tall buildings that is, in fact, already standard practice in many offices—but without the banner of the name that Johnson supplies. Form and materials now follow performance. Computers have hypnotized the architectural imagination, and performative criteria are fueling an accelerating use of the computer that is allowing architects to conceive and construct buildings of a complexity that was impracticable or even impossible to build not very long ago. Architects now enlist a variety of programs not just as pencils, but as black boxes with algorithms that bring the programs' own proclivities, talents and IQs to a design: even sketching on a digital pad has consequences profoundly different from sketching on a sheet of paper. Programs are not innocent; they have prejudice; they are programmed to address their own program.

Most recently, at the extreme end of this emerging paradigm, some architects have identified parametrics as a messianic agent capable of restructuring the entire discipline with a new, binding unitary philosophy that ties it all together. Parametrics has even achieved the status of an "ism," parametricism having been proposed as architecture's own string theory. Though parametrics may be the tipping point in a growing number of computer-savvy offices, in "Performative Skyscraper," Johnson takes a broader view, nesting parametrics within a larger picture that posits that form generation results from data-driven optimization, a practice that has always been followed in architecture. The difference now, however, is that with computational tools, the quantitative knowability of a building is verifiable across many environmental and constructive issues, and the knowability has superseded the indeterminacy of qualitative logic: hard data trump soft theory and history. Architectural design can now enjoy the aura and comfort of fact.

For Johnson, Grasshopper, the program, is not the Darwinian summum in an evolutionary march of the fittest algorithms, but part of a wider logic of performance long rationalized and optimized in so many arenas that collectively they can add up to the logic behind building designs that behave as organisms, from the window wall, to air handling systems, to the city, at all scales.

In a thorough roll-out of recent and not-so-recent architectural case histories spanning the globe, Johnson proposes performativity as an operational basis and theoretical armature for current architectural practice, based on newly accessible measurability, higher performance levels, and advanced computational design tools. He builds his case incrementally, project by project, scrupulously maintaining an objective neutrality, accumulating the evidence about performativity without challenging the logic of any specific design. He rests his case on the critical mass of the scores of efforts he cites. He does not erode the thesis by challenging any of the case studies as projects, but cites them primarily for their performativity: he is simply acknowledging facts on the ground, the evidence that the field is changing substantially, even without much directive intentionality on the part of architects. The programs keep on coming.

With digital algorithms encouraging higher degrees of performance, the empiricism of data is taking the place of more abstract theory, shifting the field to a new paradigm that elevates digital instrumentality not only into a design system but also into a de facto value in itself.

Johnson focuses on the high-rise because the phenomenon is most pronounced and obvious where so many energy and sustainability demands make the skyscraper the obvious terrain where performativity is most urgent and rewarding—where the necessity of performativity is most manifest. In the high-rise designs that he analyzes, performance has been rationalized and optimized in so many arenas that cumulatively performance drives many aspects of the whole design, from the window wall, to environmental systems, to social spaces and infrastructure. He elevates performativity beyond its status as an operational baseline that can be monitored by a building superintendent to its status as a system of thought structuring architectural practice. If performativity works at the scale of a skyscraper, it can work at any scale.

In focusing on the high-rise, he is also leveling a critique at a building type that has been so standardized that few offer pleasant, humanistic environments, despite marble-festooned lobbies and spectacular iconic forms that signal otherwise. Tens of thousands of run-of-the-mill high-rises are exercises in maximizing minima, the bleakest among them failing to offer sensory stimulation and social support. When high-rises rise higher, multiplication tables kick in with ever greater urgency and intransigence, crowding out exceptions to the rule, confirming the well-known, well-exercised skyscraper typology that makes a necessity out of the common box. As buildings grow taller and bigger, a logic of optimization inexorably takes over design calculus, so that moments and qualities that architects might propose in smaller buildings—an eruption in the grid, a pause in space, regularity graduating toward diversity, poetic stanzas—fall victim to value engineering.

Over the history of the high-rise, especially in the 20th century, the process of multiplication that leads to standardization has been deterministic and often mean, supported by America's long-standing respect for the Fordist model: efficiency is a culture and an imperative. Like their distant 19th century ancestor, the Crystal Palace, most high-rises are built like factories out of repetitive, standardized parts in assembly-line fashion. Major and minor cities around the world have become crowded with exercises in repetition that banalize high-rise structures that might otherwise elevate the life and spirit of cities. Instead of being aspirational, the high-rise is served flat and dry. Identifying performativity as a basis for evaluating design and the environment, Johnson is alerting architects to new tools with which to operate on, and transform, the building type, to invent a gentler, kinder, more inspired skyscraper environment. Talking performativity is subversive in that architects may now approach design with arguments about optimization that will allow them to operate more creatively in a bottom-line context by proposing a more profitable bottom line: arguing for greater profits may dovetail with ways of designing better buildings. Architects have a new, very potent arrow in their design quiver when they use the computer to identify environmental issues and design the architecture of its engineering. They can reassert the design control over the high-rise that they lost when they became exterior decorators, relegated to areas like the skin.

Potentially the tools may restore wonder to a building type that no one any longer cranes his neck to see. The issue now is how to make extreme verticality a humanizing experience instead of an alienating condition.

The age-old desire to occupy the sky and look back down on earth started with the biblical Tower of Babel, and first took form in Middle Eastern ziggurats, continuing later with medieval towers, Gothic spires and Renaissance campaniles. In modern times, the Woolworth, Chrysler, and Empire State buildings, all taller than any biblical dream, had the "magic to stir men's blood," in Daniel Burnham's phrase. They followed Louis Sullivan's dictum to "be every inch a proud and soaring thing, rising in sheer exultation from bottom to top." But the monotony that has resulted from the drive to economy diminishes the experience of an Icarus building type that, theoretically, should be exciting because it pierces the clouds, reaches for the sky and challenges gravity. The quantitative has defeated the qualitative as aspiration has succumbed to a deflationary spiral of reduced expectation and monotony. Like Icarus, the skyscraper once soared but has since fallen, at least in common practice.

Most unfortunately, space itself, the building block of architecture, is straightjacketed within a typology that has become rote; "space" is filtered through a sequence of minimizations. The usually planimetric building type, conceived to be flat in plan and elevation, is extruded, gridded, pancaked, cored, tubed, sealed and essentially closed not only to the outside but also closed within itself, compartmentalized in the striations of stacked floors. The on-going race to build a new generation of spectacular super-tall structures, each a spectacle of adrenal height, iconic presence and effective advertising, has done little to challenge the prevalent typology of the point tower as an exercise in deterministic optimization sheathed in an apologetically elegant skin. The high-rise persistently resists challenge because of the underlying calculus of efficiency and profit motive.

In "Performative Skyscraper," Johnson, who has designed many high-rises in America and abroad (increasingly in Asia), has identified a phenomenon that, like a force, is disrupting the logic that has long determined the form and ethos of the high-rise. He maintains that based on performance analysis, the computer can now enhance and transform the typology so that the buildings achieve high levels of efficiency in multiple arenas of function, some seldom addressed effectively. Those areas can be multiple and simultaneous so that performativity is compounded, cross-referenced and integrated.

The irony of his argument is that it does not challenge the old calculus of optimized efficiency as a determinant of form, but turns the logic on itself by proposing a computer-assisted methodology that is even more optimizing by a whole order of magnitude, displacing the machine-based calculus of efficiency of an earlier era. We are now seeing buildings that we've never seen before, and performance-driven, computer-enabled logic is a large factor in an emerging sea-change. Computers are not used for immediate form generation but for performance optimization, and form results from performance. Performativity as a driver of design holds great promise for enriching our built environment.

Technology in architecture is often treated as the servant of design, not the driver. But sometimes technology overtakes theory, coming unexpectedly from behind through the back door. In his Yale lectures, architecture historian Vincent Scully pointed out that in the 19th century, the cast iron train shed deferred politely to the classicized world in front, where travelers stepped into vast triumphal volumes of space as civic as any Roman bath. In Paris and London, classically designed facades and halls front the grand train stations, creating a dignified, ceremonial introduction to the working train sheds in back.

But after World War I, the logic of the sheds—minimal amount of materials spanning and covering maximal amounts of space—overtook the classical frontispiece, becoming the architecture itself. The First World War basically killed any lasting mythology of classicism, and in architecture, the machine—in the form of new building—overtook the classical orders to establish a new order. Johnson is identifying a similar phenomenon today, that of a newer machine doing the same, taking over from the back room where the computer has already been applied to many aspects of design. A post-mechanical machine is taking over the logic of construction, and inspiration, better coordinating efforts across many disciplines. Johnson dignifies instrumentality with theory, elevating building performativity from operation to concept, from a class to a phylum.

Johnson is a practicing architect, and perhaps because he writes about architecture from within the studio, he analyses architecture as process as well as result. As Samuel Mockbee, founder of the Rural Studio, once said, you're not truly an architect until you've been sued, and in his introduction, Johnson credits the reflections that his Museum Tower in Dallas cast on the skylights of the nearby Nasher Museum with spurring his office into researching more fully how glass performs. Their research into the behavior of reflections and the technology of glass gave Johnson the impetus for the book, much expanded by the experience of other architects in other buildings. His basic perception is that design is a verb that begets a consequent verb, that design can be understood as analyzing the behavior of a building, and that the result can obey set parameters within a dynamic environment of change. The paradigm is behaviorist, and it tolerates and perhaps encourages complex forms that supersede the unitary geometries that have characterized architecture since Plato.

Today the game has changed since the time an architect did a seminal sketch and other architects developing the ideas into a set of drawings. Now architects as well as specialists interact simultaneously in a dynamic design process, with the goal of creating a building that performs optimally according to many criteria. If classical buildings were conceived in the image of Platonic ideals, existing in a kind of changeless eternity, performative buildings are conceived as creatures of change, operating within an acceptable and optimized range of behavior. They are deeply post-classical, conceived in a constant becoming rather than at a point of stasis.

Rotating in the anti-gravitational, non-directional space of a glowing screen, computer-generated images are hypnotic, and like a charismatic person, the computer galvanizes the design process in ways that are, nonetheless, often subtle and unclear. Computer software is not a neutral or transparent medium, but one with prejudice latent in the DNA of the programs. Software can contest the will of the architect with a will of its own without ever letting on that there's a contest. Johnson says that architects in his office have tested programs against each other to see if different buildings result from the use of different programs, and they claim that differences are minor, and that different programs gravitate to a common mean instead of polarizing to extremes.

It is not that the performance of a building has never been factored into the design of a building before. Johnson makes clear that whether or not form actually followed function for much of the 20th century, performativity has long been a basis for design. Since the embrace of 3D computer modeling in architecture schools and offices, the instrumentality of the computer—its operative character as a tool and a brain— has played an implicitly and explicitly generative role in shaping design, and program by program, computational design has been gaining momentum over analog design.

Johnson's thesis is that performativity as an ideology has superseded Deconstructivist theory, which itself superseded Post-Modernism's emphasis on history, which had displaced the tenets of machined Modernism as the new driver of design.

As an architect interested in what might be called a hands-on process of design, Johnson explains his cases from real-life examples, inducing principles from example rather than deducing from precepts. His methodology is pragmatic and empirical, based in a real-life laboratory of experience and practice that deals with wind loads, wind harvesting, energy conservation and many other environmental issues. The prominence of sustainability in a world sensitized to global warming and extreme weather has given pragmatic urgency to the position.

Though Johnson derives his lessons from practice, he never mentions his own buildings but ecumenically identifies contemporary buildings by other architects around the world that exemplify issues: the resulting panorama forms a contemporary history around the subject. With encyclopedic range, he draws from whichever buildings and practices best illustrate his points. Johnson's text is dense, packed and tersely engineered: he never mentions the same fact twice. The manifesto is gentle and inductive rather than deductive, graduating from the bottom up.

With this book, Johnson joins a lineage of architects and authors dealing with the subject, including Louis Sullivan, who wrote "The Tall Office Building Artistically Considered, "and Ada Louise Huxtable, who authored "The Tall Building Artistically Reconsidered."

"Performative Skyscraper" also follows Johnson's own first book, "Tall Building: Imagining the Skyscraper," in which he discusses the skyscraper as a cultural artifact. His current book is instead an attempt to theorize the impact of the computer on architecture by discussing the many preconditions and precedents that ramped up to what is now its full integration in standard practice. He foregrounds a largely back-grounded subject as it has emerged into professional consciousness, placing the operations of the computer front and center, especially its digestive capacity to handle and shape vast amounts of data relating to disparate building systems. In the design studio, coordinating and hybridizing the systems adds up to buildings that are, in the abstract, the resultant of the computational analyses. Johnson organizes the book thematically in five chapters, starting with the many ways of considering buildings built up around natural phenomena such as the sun, daylight, wind, and seismic forces, each ecosystem striving to optimize energy consumption and sustainability. Both are subjects of major importance to the public at large and to building occupants and owners.

Originally motivated to further research the behavior of glass skins because of his experience in Dallas at Museum Tower, Johnson elaborates on the many approaches to shape curtain walls as performative skins, including coatings, fritting, screens, double-walls, and photovoltaics. He adds wind-energy capture and more exotic solutions such as vegetated walls to the options of how to clad and accessorize a tower: Johnson includes many new, up-to-date variants on enclosure that add to known skins. Johnson extrapolates from the eco-technology of the high-rise to the communities within and outside the building: no building is an island. In courts of law, to test an argument, judges sometimes take the logic to its extreme, to see if it holds. Johnson does the same with the concept of performativity, taking it beyond the building, into the neighborhood and the city, on the assumption that the building is a building block of each. Johnson tests his thesis at all scales, "from the spoon to the city," in Ernesto Rogers' phrase.

But the core of the book turns on his explanation of parametric design, the new game-changing kid on the block that has attracted considerable design attention (and promotion). Parametrics as an algorithmic process of establishing measurable parameters for performance inside and outside a building has been enabled by new computer programs that have made parametrics a force in the field. Whether on the skin of a building or within its body, the programs allow and even breed a formal complexity that enables optimization. The complexity is not generated for the sake of expressive form but as vehicles of efficiency for selected functions. The programs tend toward complexity rather than simplicity because the building is conceived as a dynamic three-dimensional field of variable environmental forces that break with geometric purity. No longer is each façade of even a four-sided tower systematically the same; each side is designed to react optimally to its own orientation. The design process is not driven by theory or aesthetics, but by the empirical standards of how to make a building work, and how to optimize performance. Perhaps the most obvious moment of "performance" in a building is the envelope that separates the inside from the elements. Johnson begins his book by focusing on the many ways of making the skin of a high-rise perform optimally per various selected criteria.

A great limitation of high-rise design has been its focus on the skin, a practice confirmed by the prejudice of certain digital programs toward surface rather than volume and space. Given the assumed typology and point-of-departure of the high-rise as a box-like point tower, designing a glass skin wrapping a tall prism is the default position. No doubt against their wishes and training, architects have become exterior decorators who have effectively given up on the rest of the building, especially on spatiality, to become shape makers. Chinese central business districts are crowded with exhibitionistic, one-liners that are hollow attempts at formal, attention-grabbing originality.

Even if some of the investigations into the performativity stay at the surface, they are exciting investigations of the skin, amounting at least to perceptual transformations of the high-rise through the creation of environmental ecologies. Johnson's technique is to enumerate the many ways skin can behave, effectively changing from passive to active to performative. Skin takes on a life of its own, no longer the servant of the volume, acquiring its own logic and geometry. Under the variable forces on the façade, the skin, performatively reconsidered, is no longer so unitary, not so Cartesian. The skin may be interrupted, or erupted, or even disturbed, for environmental reasons, but the resulting effects can seem expressive and artistic, the start of a break down in the practice of high-rise design as usual.

Johnson's very well-illustrated book clearly establishes that designing the skin for performance leads to new morphologies, many of them visually persuasive and seductive: some are striking and even beautiful and become objects of desire rather than simply examples of improved function. Although Johnson spends considerable time enumerating the ecological properties of glass, his choice of buildings is not limited to glazed solutions. As Walter Benjamin said, glass lacks aura, at least in its conventional usage, and Johnson's examples frequently combine glass with other materials and approaches, sometimes in double facades or integrated into exoskeletal brise-soleils.

The ways in which architects have handled the skin as a membrane and ecosystem in high-rises are strikingly different, even if each has the same goal of optimizing the membrane. In London, each façade of Kohn Pedersen Fox's Heron Tower in Bishopsgate is different from the other, one expressing its lateral steel structure, while others are programmatically articulate, simply glazed, or armored with photo-voltaic panels. The architects hybridize High-Tech style with what might be called Eco-Tech, in a mutually compatible architectural fusion. In Los Angeles Johnson cites the CalTrans building by Thom Mayne of Morphosis for a perforated metal skin fixed several inches from the interior weather wall, creating a buffering environmental cavity between the two. By separating the two walls, Mayne reinvented the eco-mechanics of the skin, dividing the work load between the two skins so that no one membrane had to perform all functions. The metal sunscreen, with operating panels animate the surface in changing, unpredictable patterns,. Mayne integrates photovoltaics on the fourth (south) service wall to capture energy.

In London Norman Foster designed the toroidal shape of Swiss Re Tower (aka the "Gherkin") to reduce wind loads and structural demands; inside, a spiral of open common break-out terraces creates exceptional spaces where office workers can socialize. In Abu Dhabi, the elegant Al Bahr Towers by Aedas Architects is encrusted with a triangulated exoskeletal growth of environmentally responsive panels that spread over parts of the facade, opening and closing with solar and daylighting demands. The skin recalls traditional mashrabiya, wood lattices that shade while admitting air and affording visual privacy.

Some of his examples, such as the Bahrain World Trade Center Tower, by Atkins, and the Pearl River Tower in Guangdong, China, by SOM, are aerodynamically contoured for wind loads and include wind-driven turbines for capturing the energy of the wind. Among the collection that Johnson has curated are towers designed to be vertical farms, which achieve their ecological value with deeply terraced facades that serve as planting trays within an overall structure that looks forested top to bottom. Johnson shows many approaches for creating skins that are effectively ecosystems.

The reconsideration of the skin as a responsive membrane that acts and reacts to the sun, wind and views may have formal consequences, but the responses are not essentially formalist. Rather than form for the sake of form, performative criteria shape the facades. But the criteria need not simply be the environmental physics prevailing in a place. Johnson broadens the notion of what a skin might be by enumerating ways in which the surface of a building can be occupied. Among Malaysian architect Ken Yeang's facades are vertical fields populated by people on terraced shelves where vegetation grows. Cross breezes blow through and up. Yeang dimensionalizes the façade by creating biomimetic environments. He brings the logic inside where the floor plate is designed to maximize ecological benefit, while the exterior extends the living space into the environment. Outside and inside blur. Johnson's thesis of performative architecture is anti-formalist in that there is no preconceived notion of form, a box or otherwise. The form is instead generated by activity and reactive response within and outside the building, or in the confrontational conditions where inside and outside meet.

In many cases the technology that takes over the facades, whether simple or complex, changes the perception of the building as well as its performance. A century ago, the machine inspired many Modernist buildings as a metaphor and building process, but this time the machine is less linear and more organic, the creation of a second machine age that is digital rather than mechanical: instead of static fixity, computer-based designs can now operate with a digital intelligence capable of changeable, dynamic behavior.

In Frankfurt, the Berlin firm Sauerbruch Hutton dimensionalized the façade of the KfW Westarkade office building with a polychromatic exoskeleton akin to Le Corbusier's brise-soleils. Corb of course said that buildings were machines for living in, and though the brise-soleils of his Unités d'Habitation were performative, cutting sun exposure, creating shade and inviting occupation, newer versions such as the apparatus on the KfW Westarkade are operative and organic, changing heliotropically: the panels covering the entire façade change orientation as the sun and weather change. In the former Modernst paradigm, the brise-soleil is fixed and static; in the new paradigm, the shades are reactive and dynamic. Both paradigms "perform," but each in a different way.

For Johnson, discussions of the skin are simply a first step in challenging the accepted typology of the high-rise as a closed environmental system. He uses skin as the start of a critique of established high-rise typology.

The skyscraper is, with few exceptions, basically a point tower, one of the most restrictive building types. It is necessary and appropriate for Johnson to address the ecosystem of the membrane not only because it is the type's most actively transactional component, mediating between outside and inside, but also because it is one of the few negotiable aspects of a building type that is, in actual practice, otherwise predetermined—and even over-determined. Strangely, the manipulation of the skin is not in and of itself transformative to the point tower: it just looks transformed. It may be the first challenge to the typology, but the challenge is hardly decisive.

Custom, cost and physics have conspired to make the high-rise a restrictive building type that tends to physical closure. Air conditioning systems traditionally demanded the building be sealed. Engineers often thought of the building as a structural tube, another step toward closure. Economies of construction demanded that a floor plate be extruded up the shaft, resulting in a pancaked structure. The economics of repetition have favored uniformity. Developers have generally preferred column-free spaces centered on an elevator core that behaves structurally, a morphology that tends to favor symmetry. The usually planimetric building type, conceived to be flat in plan and elevation, has been extruded, gridded, and pancaked, and essentially closed not only to the outside but also closed within itself, compartmentalized. The on-going race to build a new generation of spectacular super-tall structures, each a spectacle of adrenal height, iconic presence and effective advertising, has done little to challenge the prevalent typology of the point tower as an exercise in deterministic optimization. The high-rise has persistently resisted challenges because of the calculus of compounded efficiencies.

The demands of this design environment tend to compress space, which is effectively defenseless against all the physical encroachments. Metaphorically, the key for "space" is missing on computer keyboards, and therefore absent from arguments constructed around the computer.

One distinguished precedent that would greatly enrich any discussion about tall buildings is Paul Rudolph's mid-rise structure, the Art and Architecture Building at Yale (now Paul Rudolph Hall). The A + A Building of 1963 is mostly overlooked as a spatial paradigm because it fell out of polite, acceptable discourse with the onset of Post-Modernism, disparaged and even denigrated for decades.

But in this seven-story midrise, flowing space is the driver. Rudolph expands and contracts heights and widths, using floors like pistons to create over 30 different levels within a building whose elevators stop at only seven floors. Space is graduated so incrementally that occupants often choose to walk up or down a few steps rather than take a ride to the floors accessed by the elevator. Space itself, conceived in vectorial flows, becomes a positive, a void cast as a presence rather than an absence, keeping form at bay. Rudolph's spaces are empowered rather than defenseless. The interiors become vertical landscapes.

Rudolph broke the box in the Z dimension, doing what his architectural mentor, Frank Lloyd Wright had done in the horizontal dimension when he stretched his buildings into the prairie. Rudolph's genius was simply to take the plan of the Prairie houses—Taliesin East, for example, or the Robie House—and rotate the plan upright 90 degrees, so that Wright's lessons applied to the high-rise in a way Wright never did. Wright's horizontal porosity became Rudolph's vertical porosity.

In short, Rudolph excavated space in the morphologically dense and stubborn typology of the high-rise, thick with floors and spatially striated, and his sectional intentions, with all their potential for breeding socializing interior spaces, help break open exterior form. The discontinuity of the skin, with deep crevasses and strong, declarative pylons, keeps the building from being closed, sealed unitary volumes.

Rudolph breaks the container even at a much larger scale in his Asian projects. In a vast retail-office-residential complex in Singapore he uses modular parts ingeniously pieced together as terraces, balconies and rooftops to open the box. The "skins" of his buildings are occupied by people. He sometimes hybridizes small and tall structures in complex, interpenetrating masses that form mixed-use composites. Space is not a consequence of form but instead a vector opening form to diversified functions.

Single use tends to breed unified form, while mixed uses tends to diversity form. Mixing the uses opens up the system with other typologies—shopping, for example—which has been an especially disruptive force in high-rise buildings in China and the Far East, where shopping can be an air-conditioned blood sport. These uses often reach many stories up the base of the high-rise, sometimes leaping across tall buildings via bridges.

Dutch architect Rem Koolhaas introduced a version of Rudolph's spatiality when he famously discussed the section of the Downtown Athletic Club in "Delirious New York," where the sectional heights vary to accommodate a mixture of uses. Koolhaas, who has written at length about shopping as an international phenomenon, talks about diversity inside high-rises in terms of program, and in his text, Johnson takes the comment about program further, treating it as an indicator of the building's behavioral performance. But both Koolhaas and Johnson avoid space as a subject in itself, only confirming that the typology of the high-rise has reduced the importance and presence of space to the status of the area sandwiched between striations.

If Koolhaas disrupts the high-rise typology with the diversifying force of program, Sir Norman Foster uses structure to loosen its tight grip. The value in Foster's use of structure is not for its display of technology but for its ability to open spaces to create public rooms that socialize buildings. The Hearst Corporation Headquarters in New York is one of the rare high-rises with a vast public space in which the occupants regularly gather, as though in a town square. Foster frequently creates these spaces throughout the shaft of a high-rise, not simply at the base or at the top. At Swiss Re in London, the curvilinear form of the "gherkin" reduces the wind load, while a spiral of interior terraces wind up through the building, creating socializing spaces within the tower.

Foster also re-arranges high-rise infrastructure, opening the normally stacked and closed interiors. By placing the elevator cores at the perimeter of his buildings—at the four corners of the Hong Kong and Shanghai Bank Headquarters in Hong Kong, or at the three points of a triangle, as at the Commerzbank in Frankfurt—Foster liberates the center of the buildings and creates atria, which give occupants common space with the environmental benefits of light and circulating air. At Frankfurt, the tall atrium acts as a chimney that draws air up through the stack from four story terraces placed among the stacks. As in many examples cited by Johnson, Foster poses the dilemma of the chicken and the egg. Did inventing the structure and re-organizing the infrastructure create the opportunity for interior public space or did the desire for urban space demand structural and infrastructural re-invention?

Johnson notes that performativity predates the extensive use of the computer, and many of the projects that Johnson cites really belong to periods when the computer was not yet driving architecture as a force of change, and architects were using languages other than performance to guide their thinking. Johnson mentions the Max Reinhardt House that Peter Eisenman designed in Berlin, a twisted, Expressionist version of a Mobius strip springing from one high-rise shaft in an arch to a second shaft, anticipating by decades the CCTV tower of Rem Koolhaas in Beijing. Eisenman was not yet designing with computers, and Koolhaas has never let the computer set his conceptual agenda. Eisenman was dealing with "weak," indeterminate form and challenging normative design and Cartesian geometry, while Koolhaas was interested in creating a tower of parallel public and professional transportation systems inside that journeyed through the striated section.

Neither had harnessed the powers of the computer to push his thinking beyond the exigencies of structure. However, the idea of a two-point tower each tower bridged to the other at the top would inform the radical proposal by United Architects for its 9/11 competition entry. The tower declared a new agenda for the high-rise, and certainly one based on performativity as negotiated by the computer.

The group of architects used the computer to completely transform the received typology of the point tower in what they proposed as a concatenation of leaning, bulging, walking towers fused at the upper levels in Siamese relationships. The concepts that drove Eisenman and Koolhaas before landed here in an arena of active computational invention. The notions of ecosystems and sustainability did not generate the vision, even though the vision recursively supported each. The concept of conjoined, leaning towers, linked with skywalks serving as urban streets, was among the most daring proposals of its time, an early result of computer-generated design and an exercise in morphing applied at daringly large scale. While rethinking what a high-rise could be, and using the computer to push the envelope literally and figuratively, the architects scrupulously kept the floor plates efficient and within the parameters demanded by developers. It seemed possible to imagine that the density of inhabitants in the multiple towers could support a street in the upper reaches where the towers merge.

Again, the chicken or the egg? Did the architects want the building to perform as an urban space, or did the form create the opportunity for the urban space?

Challenges to the high-rise typology have taken many forms before the computer, but none constituted a transformative approach for reconsidering skyscraper design: economy prevailed, cemented in practice. But in a building type where scale is a multiplier, performance matters, and Johnson has identified a way of thinking that at last promises to empower architects and insinuate itself into practice by front-loading economies of material, construction and the environment into the design equation. That the computer can confirm optimization through measurement grounds the approach in reassuring data. The bottom line—the sum total of data on energy consumption, acoustics, structural efficiency, lighting, traffic flows— becomes clear and actionable. You can take the data to the bank for a construction loan.

Johnson's third chapter, the core of his book, deals with the advent of parametric programs, which tip the field rapidly toward performativity as a design system and theory. Performance goals for energy, structural efficiency and environmental comfort can be modeled parametrically, dialed so that the resultant designs are not simply formed, but informed, and data-rich. Each project entails a process of mining and evaluating data.

Performative data-driven design is very different from theory-driven design, where buildings are textualized with cultural issues meant to be "read" and interpreted. In Johnson's paradigm of performativity, "driving" a design is a more apt metaphor than "reading" a design. In the context of the rapidly evolving and expanding use of the computer in architectural design, parametrics takes on added and pivotal importance, triggering an integrative approach made possible by digital networking.

Perhaps the most vocal figure promoting parametric design today is Patrik Schumacher, an associate architect at Zaha Hadid Architects who has authored books on parametrics and who escalates the parametric argument with ambitious claims. If Johnson writes with understatement, Schumacher champions parametrics as a unitary theory. The architect has been a driving force behind high-rise design in Hadid's office, which has produced an entire generation of tall structure designs characterized by a fluid verticality whose sinuous lines frequently contain structure and carry building systems. Some of the designs are twin or multiple towers that fuse in their upper reaches, forming public spaces in their overlap; some splay and splash at the bottom, again creating public spaces as the vertical mass spreads horizontally into the city. Like Frank Gehry, who has pioneered architectural revolution in low- and midrise buildings, Hadid and Schumacher have had trouble reinventing the high-rise, recasting lower buildings that they can spatialize horizontally. The morphology of the pancake stack interferes.

Johnson embeds a second narrative about performativity within his text when he outlines the position taken by Schumacher. In his own writings, Schumacher goes well beyond Johnson's position to philosophize on parametric design. Even though Johnson writes that parametric practices "substitute more quantitative thinking for formerly esoteric design strategies," Schumacher embraces the esoteric.

In what Johnson calls a Eurocentric argument, Schumacher espouses that parametric style represents a new "unified theory" in the tradition of the unified theories espoused by Alberti in his "Ten Books on Architecture," by Durand in his discourses on neoclassic architecture, and by Le Corbusier in "Towards a New Architecture." Surprisingly Schumacher's rather prideful argument is not based on instrumentality: he does not compare the advent of the computer to the advent of paper and moveable type, or the advent of the wooden models of Renaissance architecture, so influenced by studies of human anatomy. Schumacher's argument is ontological rather than empirical.

Perhaps staking out an original position in contradistinction to architects of an older generation, Schumacher argues that architecture practiced parametrically should be practiced purely, ignoring any issues that take architecture outside its proper subjects. His argument echoes Clement Greenberg's argument about the separation of arts that should be practiced purely, but Schumacher recites more contemporary theory, invoking "autopoiesis," a term applied in systems theory that was first used by biologists to define the self-maintaining chemistry of living cells. The cell—like Schumacher's parametrically-designed building—exists and evolves as a system of interacting networks in an ongoing dynamic of self-generation and transformation. Whether a cell or a building, the system is self-contained and closed. Schumacher admits no outside discourse such as politics or philosophy or art in a system that is self-referential and closed.

Counter-intuitively, his argument occurs within the context of Hadid's practice. From the very beginning of her career, painting influenced Hadid's design, opening up her architectural system: the paintings produced a hybrid vigor that fortified the vision. She did not operate within a closed architectural and intellectual system. The same might be said of Frank Gehry, who was deeply influenced by the space and light artists who worked in Gehry's milieu in Venice, California.

That Schumacher is now arguing for the autopoiesis of the field is self-contradictory because Hadid has always operated within an open architectural frame. Schumacher himself described the leading corners of the Vitra Fire Station design as a cluster of three volumes in forced perspectives that diverged and disagreed, each vanishing to different points: the architects had created an optical environment inspired by the painted spatial irrationalities of the Russian Suprematists around World War I. The idea for a landscape of moving platforms in Hadid's entry in the Parc de la Villette competition in 1983 came from looking at Jacques Tinguely's sculpture, with its moving parts.

Hadid opened the system by grafting the discourse of another field to architecture, and the power of the work has always been in its freedoms and open, asymmetrical forms. Under the influence of Schumacher's theories, Hadid's language, especially in large-scale buildings including the high-rise is tending to closed symmetries and unitary self-containment. The turn is fundamental.

Wolf Prix, principle of Coop Himmelblau, maintains that any system, including architecture, must stay open and receptive to change, otherwise, according to thermodynamic law, the system itself will die. He insistently maintains that architects who only think about Vitruvius, Palladio and Schinkel—that is, architectural history—will only produce Vitruvius, Palladio and Schinkel. The system expires. Prix has explicitly based his architecture on open systems that allow and even invite outside agents and systems to enter the design process, triggering random fluctuations and an ongoing process of feedback loops. He believes an open system that can handle random fluctuations is robust, self-repairing and self-organizing and results in a decentralization of all the system's components. This is the post-classical position: parts do not belong in prescribed positions within a set ordination.

The recently completed high-performance aluminum skin of the Coop Himmelblau's brilliant Dalian Conference Center, with gills strategically placed to open for light and air, was designed with a parametric program. But Prix maintains that parametrics alone is a too linear process, and that it must be folded into a stop-and-go iterative process of trial and error that stirs the building into a multi-valent complexity allowing the building to perform in many ways, not just a few. He maintains that this process keeps the building from becoming a linear and literal one-liner derived from a single logic. Prix folds mistakes in his design process as a matter of principle.

If Schumacher's arguments are philosophically ambitious, Johnson more modestly and credibly explains parametrics as a form of design research; and, taken as operational procedure, parametrics is easier to digest without the price of the 'religion' that Schumacher attaches to it. But while Johnson limits his book to the subject at hand, staying on-message, Johnson himself admits other issues are at play: "the determinants of exceptional architecture remain elusive."

Indeed. The elephant in the room is the nagging issue of the role of the architect in a data-driven search for design implemented by programs narrowly scripted for optimizing such performance goals as daylighting, ventilation, acoustics, energy use and structure. Performative design is driven by numbers and optimization, and the deterministic process minimizes the role of the architect as a trained, intuitive intelligence bringing belief systems other than efficiency and efficacy to the keyboard. When Johnson lists buildings, he describes them only, or mostly, from the point of view of performativity. He stays on-message.

There are other logics that Johnson suggests, though admirably he contains his subject. But in streamlining the information, Johnson edges toward a totalizing argument. Not all these buildings were designed for performativity, but in the rearview mirror he sees them from that angle.

Still he sets up expectations that there are other criteria with which to fill the bucket. What we learned through the last thirty years from the architectural generation that came of age in the 1980s and '90s—the generation of Schumacher's mentors—is the value of complementary, contrary and independent systems, multiple systems which co-exist in states of flux and reflex, contributing to the impurity of systems. Their confrontation and hybridization deliver the unexpected. Disagreement is productive, perhaps even stimulating. Gehry and Hadid mixed art and architecture. Eisenman injected philosophy in design, and design in philosophy: his Max Reinhardt tower in Berlin is an act of indeterminacy inviting unstable readings. Tschumi made program a basis of design, and for his design for Parc de la Villette in Paris, he multiplied programs in what might be called an energy field so that spontaneous activities combust unpredictably at different times on different days in different seasons. The urban performance derives more from the lessons of performance art than from performativity. The shared etymology is merely coincidental.

Schumacher's narrow and strict, somewhat Calvinist interpretation of parametrics is not Johnson's. The California architect intimates other logics. Though Johnson cites the work of many architects in his case studies of performativity, he says the best of them are not one-note architects but designers who pursue multiple issues, in a layered process. He does not maintain that they are all ayatollas of performativity, but that their buildings bring to bear other subjects. He acknowledges that qualitative issues play their role but dwells on the quantitative, while caveating his argument. Early on he writes: "Human intelligence remains at the center of the design process, interpreting the data, directing the integration of goals and recalibrating them into conceptual solutions. Thanks to computers, parameters can be accurately programmed, tracked and measured but the determinants of exceptional architecture remain elusive."

He withholds full credit from performativity. He further qualifies his subject, saying, "there is often a sense in the profession that higher levels of performance equate to more compelling, or more perfectible, architecture. The term, performance, is, in fact, highly qualified and refers strictly to the satisfaction of specific parametric goals."

An architecture of performativity based on the computer's ability to maximize efficiency would seem to open itself up to the same criticism that Modernism eventually attracted, and merited, plunging architecture into decades of self-reassessment. Performativity is not so different from concepts of efficiency dating from the Progressive era; it's just a different form of maximizing efficiency within a holistic computational system. The new smart machine may seem to invite a return of the critique. Form following research into performativity would seem to be innocent, but it begs issues of scientism rather than humanism, and the specter of a new tyranny of the machine.

Johnson writes a corrective tale: it is refreshing that rather that continuing speculation on architectural metaphysics, he brings up the physics of architectural design via the computer and parametric programs. With computational tools, we can now concretely understand and visualize how forces move and interact in a building and think of design as behavior rather than object or theory. The process grounds design in a certain knowability.

But the tale is also cautionary. Parametrics promises to give so many concrete answers to so many questions that it risks becoming a new fundamentalism that marginalizes many other subjects. The quantifiable is always more easily understood than the qualitative. Numbers, however, are rarely inspired. The inspiration comes from the mathematician who arranges the numbers in certain persuasive ways.

But Johnson, though he is codifying a relatively new subject, is not claiming hegemony in the field for performativity, rather simply introducing a potent design narrative within an existing mix of narratives. Besides the ecosystems he discusses and varieties of curtain walls, he raises questions of mixed use, socializing spaces, sustainability, green facades, the city and other subjects that give added environmental dimension to performativity. He does not reduce architecture to a single issue but suggests a broader interpretation of performativity beyond data. The approach is holistic. Performativity doesn't displace theoretical criticism.

In this panorama of contemporary architecture, Johnson—in Isaiah Berlin's formulation—acts as the hedgehog rather than the fox. Johnson writes as an architect and historian who knows "one big thing" rather than many things. This is the strength of the text. In his argument about the ubiquity of performativity across the field, he extrapolates from the case studies on the premise that performativity has long been integral to the design process at all levels of design.

Architecture is at a point of no return in its acceptance of computer design which now subsumes parametric programs into the discipline. Johnson rests his case on the critical mass of all the efforts he has cited. He does not erode the thesis by challenging any of the case studies, or the reasoning behind them. Nor is he hard-selling performativity as the new modus operandi. He is documenting and describing a phenomenon that has appeared irreversibly in the field, and is poised to take over a significant role in the design process. He writes with a certain detachment and distance, not as an exponent but as an observer. He scrupulously maintains a neutrality as author, following a policy of documenting the evidence with fact and photograph.

What is impressive and even fascinating about the phenomenon is that rather than espousing new forms or even new tenets, Johnson has announced a design process that is based on a dynamic process. With advocating a computational approach to design, he outlines simply a methodology and a path of invention within webbed systems that cross platforms and programs. Data drive the design in a fluid process of research, and the method makes no a priori assumption of form or typology, but instead yields design through building streams of information. The process enables an architect to become something of an engineer operating within a fluid field of open consultation.

The process is a procedural analog to the design of many buildings in the last two decades that take their inspiration from energy and flow fields. Projects like the Parc de la Villette are non-hierarchical designs that privilege dynamic systems as a basis of design rather than static platonic geometries. An architecture of performativity is designed in a field of flux. The computer operates in its own field of flux.

A note of hesitation throughout the text is that the building might be charted and designed as the sum total of all the environmental forces bearing on the building. But the captain of a new ship needs to know how to interpret the data and the charts and know where to steer it, which direction to take. The design can't just be a passive resultant of input. But the designer also has to bring to bear a value system with which to steer the process and choose a destination. Just what does an architect want a building to be? The brilliant instrumentality of the computer doesn't lift the onus of responsibility from the architect. Data might be objective, and values might be subjective, but judgment is necessary to plot a course between the two.

The fame of the Tower of Babel rests in its height, and over the last several decades cities have built ever taller buildings to capture the title of the world's tallest building, echoing the biblical precedent and man's desire to live in the sky. But what is frequently forgotten in the tale is that the tower of Babel—at least in the famous Breughal interpretation, among others—was circled by a wide spiraling road that fed construction rising ever higher. The roadway also served as a common city street that was lined with structures built into the tower, and the core was honeycombed with other buildings and spaces. The tower was in fact a vertical city.

Certainly there were performative issues in building the tower, but the spiraling road is what brought the people together as a community. The technology of building the tower belonged to a skilled engineer or architect, but the wisdom lay in building a wide and accommodating road lined with spaces in and around which the citizens could meet and talk (until, of course, they couldn't). The tower was not just a multiplication table and the result of the prideful aspirations of a culture aspiring to heaven. It was a city of, for and by its citizens.

PG_22_PERFORMATIVE_SKYSCRAPER.

INTRODUCTION

The following five essays attempt to investigate the imaginative present and future of tall building design at this moment in time. I say present and future at this moment in time because some of the work we are exploring is built, some has been designed and is being built, while still other work has been designed and may or may not be built at all. Our goal has been to focus on current thinking with regard to advanced tall building design and this has led us into the present and the theoretical future. In some cases, we have gone back into the recent past in order to establish the context for where we are today. This approach has also necessarily led us away from attention to the very tallest recorded buildings or buildings which are recycling conventional design principles. While tall building design, as architects know, is an unfolding legacy of accumulated knowledge, it finds its place in the history of the type for what it invents and how it foretells the development of the next generation of tall buildings as architecture.

Why the title, PERFORMATIVE SKYSCRAPER, to capture this moment? Marc Schiler, an architect and professor at the University of Southern California's School of Architecture proposes a definition of performative: "In architecture, a performative facade is one which brings about an event, by its very existence, such as automatic shielding from the sun, or lighting an adjacent space or rejecting certain wavelengths."[1] In addition to a definition like Schiler's which speaks to certain mechanics of performance, the performative in our title refers to a broader trend in the architectural community to see design as multi-functional and measurable. This is particularly true in tall building design owing to the scale of its enterprise and the importance assigned therein to achieving high levels of performance. This state of affairs is, encouraged by the presence of the computer, in particular, parametric practices, which work to share information, deconstruct former architectural hierarchies and substitute more quantitative thinking for formerly esoteric design strategies. Additionally, the language of today's overwhelming interest in sustainability and energy management is measured in levels of performance. Whatever else might matter to architects in the design of tall buildings, performativity is today's signature theme.

I emphasize that our mission is to capture a sense of the most thoughtful work in tall building architecture because, notwithstanding the drawn-out pace of planning, capital formation, design and construction which characterize this building type, the pace of new ideas is always brisk, constantly delivering new developments. Both technical innovations and cultural trends appear on the scene with lightning speed and quickly become the subject matter of new developments in vertical building. As recently as 2008 in *TALL BUILDING: IMAGINING THE SKYSCRAPER*[2], I wrote about this building type as a cultural artifact, situated in a historical context and freighted with symbols and semiotics. Following a series of Post-World War II cultural and artistic developments which described an eventual flight from and subsequent return, to Modernism, by the end of the century, theoretical criticism appeared to many observers to have overtaken historicism as the lingua franca for establishing signification in architecture. Today, I would suggest, performativity has become that central medium.

In the writing of the first book, I was predominantly concerned with the role tall buildings played within systems of cultural relevance. Also, it seemed clear that the idea of tall buildings spoke to particular topics of our public consciousness. Chapter 1, *The Inevitable Skyscraper*, Chapter 4, *Designer Skyscraper* and Chapter 5, *FutureTall* in that book situated the tall building within a culturally and commercially-oriented motivational field, drawing likenesses between certain tall buildings and luxury goods in a retail-driven marketplace of desire and consumption. Chapter 2, *The Enrichment of Vertical Space*, which we will discuss here in new ways, looked to the genesis of expressive mixed-use towers as largely the work of a cultural avant-garde. Chapter 3, *The Environmental Skyscraper*, compared and contrasted the works of Norman Foster and Ken Yeang in an attempt to unsettle any pat assumptions of what constitutes environmental architecture and to distinguish representations of Western and Eastern ethos. The final and perhaps most freewheeling chapter, *Art Skyscrapers*, suggested a vaguely structuralist preoccupation with the archetype which many artists appear to embrace and yet express in wildly different ways through a range of media.

All this is not to say that tall buildings today are no longer actors in a cultural landscape, however, the concerns of architects and designers have, it seems to me, undergone a major shift in response to a new set of priorities. While these new priorities reflect shifting concerns within cultures at large, the vocabulary of tall buildings, the challenges they are poised to address and the criteria by which they are evaluated have changed dramatically in a short space of time. As an architect who practices, teaches and writes, I, and those around me, feel the pull of new forces in these settings as we work to investigate, explicate and design new tall buildings. Our tools are more precise and we are now asked to measure results from our buildings and weigh these measurements within a matrix of competing goals. Sometimes an unfounded presumption is detectable among our colleagues that these measurements imply a certain level of qualitative performance, that they can define overall excellence in architecture. This kind of infatuation with performativity is perhaps just the latest expression of our pervasively scientific culture which is fond of conflating science, value and morality. Our subtitle, *TALL BUILDING DESIGN NOW* acknowledges that which is obvious: that technology and our cultural responses to it are evolving so quickly that what we actually know is only what we know now. It would be hard to conceive of a conventional book with any real longevity on this topic.

In an environment in which so much can now be measured, the fields of science and engineering emphasize performance while the continuing development of digital software applications enables this emphasis. The elaboration of a window wall to reduce incident solar heat gain, the reshaping of a floor plan to reduce aerodynamic wind vortices or the creation of glass products which selectively minimize certain light wavelengths and maximize others are examples of this. In an environment in which so much information is shared, competition in the marketplace is naturally heightened and the ability to measure and record outcomes is frequently used to support claims of achievement and distinction. Where the internet and social media are the dominant models for inquiry, research, news and communications, our attention is naturally drawn to the latest and largest spectacle.

One might reasonably anticipate a reduced interest in the tall building as a topic, given a string of difficult circumstances such as the events of 9/11, the lingering global real estate recession which began in 2007, broad market trends such as the move away from institutional office space toward creative work environments and the effects of proliferating and non-place-based electronic communications. Notwithstanding these huge and influential factors, the tall building appears to endure within both industrial and post-industrial cultures. The construction of new towers continues in a wide range of locations throughout the world, although not necessarily in the original locations, while theoretical investigations, proposals and competition entries are at an all-time high, adding substance to an expanding vision of new tall buildings worldwide.

With that in mind, I have organized our investigations into five chapters which attempt to outline the most compelling aspects of tall buildings today. While each chapter could well be the basis for an entire volume, our goal is to capture the central trends going forward and summarize their impacts on the formal development of tall building architecture. We know that each topic comprises elements both visible and invisible but we have chosen to focus on those which are more visible or of a nature that they affect what is ultimately visible. In this way, and in the spirit of the earlier book, *TALL BUILDING: IMAGINING THE SKYSCRAPER*, we continue to "imagine" the skyscraper.

    Chapter One, *PERFORMATIVE ECOLOGIES*, constitutes a summary of current design activities which are directed toward producing energy-efficient and sustainable strategies in new tall buildings. These are organized around familiar natural resources such as the sun, whether concerning daylighting, heat control, photovoltaic conversion or heliostatic applications. Wind strategies are also examined through a range of formal solutions which capture wind and convert kinetic energy into electricity. Tall buildings with double skin solutions are examined which both control solar radiation and provide natural venting and air supply systems. Biomass and vertical farming are explored in a few actual installations as well as in forward-looking proposals.

    While a significant portion of Chapter One concerns the exterior enclosure systems of tall buildings, Chapter Two, *PERFORMATIVE SKINS*, focuses exclusively on these skins and attempts to identify the most advanced strategies available within the realm of established means and methods. We investigate conventional glass applications, alternative glass systems, deep skins such as rain-screens and double-wall systems. The integration of structure into the exterior skin is an emerging topic as is the recognition that with embedded electronic systems, skins can communicate in different ways and to different ends.

    Chapter Three, *PERFORMATIVE PARAMETRICS*, examines the sudden impact parametric modeling has had on the way tall buildings are designed and constructed and the external factors to which they can now respond. Rooted in traditions of ontological philosophy and expressive architectural theories dating to the 1960s, the application of digital algorithms has paved the way for measurement and optimization, highly complex form development and rapid prototyping as widespread standard procedures.

    Chapter Four, *PERFORMATIVE NEIGHBORHOODS*, returns to a topic from my earlier book, the issue of mixed-use vertical neighborhoods. While such buildings have been common in select cultures, particularly in the Far East where densities, urban land values and cultural habits support them, tall buildings in the West have generally tended toward single-use towers. This is beginning to change due to the more intense urbanization of Western cities and the tendency toward greater amenitization within vertical communities.

    Chapter Five, *PERFORMATIVE CITIES*, could be about many things, but within our purview, we identify seven international cities and the unique circumstances out of which emerge tall buildings. Our premise is that, while many of them may share technologies and protocols characteristic of the building type, each city and its particular forms of urbanization naturally lead to a unique context for tall buildings which become morphologically distinct. In a global age when our commerce, communications and lifestyles trend in the direction of homogeneity, cities constitute a kind of specificity in which tall buildings have distinctive roles. It is in these roles wherein tall buildings are required to perform, reflecting the history and socio-political context of each city.

---

[1] Schiler, Marc, *Performative Facades: A Proposed Definition*. Facade Tectonics: The Building Envelope 13, op. cit., 13.

[2] Johnson, Scott, *Tall Building: Imagining the Skyscraper*, op. cit.

CHAPTER ONE
PERFORMATIVE ECOLOGIES

Inasmuch as the high-rise tower is an inherently visible icon, and sustainability and the carbon footprint of our activities receive so much attention, the building type is now viewed through the lens of sustainability and its contribution to an overall strategy for building an energy-efficient city. A latent perception exists that the tall building is, if only by virtue of its height, an unsustainable and resource-intensive project. Considered in isolation of all other factors, this may be true, however, its embodied energy, its interactivity within a dense and mixed-use community, its prospects for re-use and redevelopment over time and the extent of its operational efficiencies are all-important ingredients in defining its overall energy impact.

If the perception of the tall building as wasteful of energy has its roots in history, many of the technical aspects of the building type which contributed to this perception were amply documented in Sigfried Giedion's *MECHANIZATION TAKES COMMAND* (1948)[3] and Reyner Banham's *THE ARCHITECTURE OF THE WELL-TEMPERED ENVIRONMENT* (1969)[4]. Early tall buildings were designed and built on the premise that energy costs were low and resources inexhaustible. Advances in lighting technology, for example were particularly important in the evolution of the building type. Gas lighting, the 19th century standard, was labor-intensive and dangerous. Edison's invention of commercially available incandescent lighting in the form of an electric lamp (1880) made the illumination of occupied space simple and safe. Floor sizes could now expand as offices were no longer required to be near a window at the building perimeter. Individualized switching allowed for flexibility in the zoning of such large floors based upon the needs of space planning.

The development of fluorescent lighting allowed the ceiling to be the source of illumination rather than the desk lamp and freed building floor plates to be even larger. The brighter fluorescent light and the fact that it provided broad ambient illumination coupled with the low price of energy allowed building floor plates to grow even larger and reduced the importance of the window wall as a source for natural light.

Only recently have LED-based fixtures become available with extraordinary brightness, accurate color rendition and long-life. Notwithstanding their high initial cost, their life-cycle costs provide enormous savings over the long term. Additionally, the combined attention given to energy efficiency and human health has had the effect of elevating the importance of maximizing natural light at the window wall. Space plans are organized such that natural light is optimized on an office floor and floor plates are configured to maximize the perimeter and limit floor depths. In certain European countries, these conditions have been prescriptively included in the building codes.

Initial developments in thermal comfort also made early towers energy-intensive. The ability to centralize heating and cooling was essential to housing large numbers of people in a single place. The earliest central heating systems provided forced air by way of wood or coal-fired furnaces. By the turn of the 20th century, radiators became common, tied to circulating systems of hot water or steam provided from a central boiler. Central air-conditioning appeared later although individual air conditioners occurred in the 1920s in certain residential and commercial buildings. The centralized HVAC systems which became dominant after World War II merged neatly with the modernist predilection for slick boxes clad in fully sealed curtain-walls which had no operable sashes and provided all environmental conditioning and ventilation by way of central systems. Intake and exhaust were consolidated and relegated to monolithic locations at the base, top or somewhere in the middle, usually flush to the window wall. As these systems were monolithic, they did not allow occupants much freedom to make individualized adjustments nor did they easily match the energy efficiencies of later more custom systems which allowed for variations in smaller comfort zones.

Finally, the provision of running water and advances in plumbing (toilets and sinks) were necessary to support the development of the tall building. By the beginning of the twentieth century, municipal water and sewage were common in tall buildings and, as with other resources, available supply of water was considered inexhaustible. Recycling or any restrictions applied to water, sewage or trash were not yet on the horizon.

Today, several tall building projects are underway worldwide which advertise their Net Zero Energy status. Is it possible to think of a tall building that generates as much energy as it has taken to produce it? Current perceptions surrounding the tall building and its prospects for achieving meaningful sustainability are colored by its extreme verticality and the sense that heavier construction and more intense mechanical systems required for pumping, lifts, heating and cooling make the building type an inherently wasteful model. Complete data is unavailable and, based on qualitative and equivocal factors such as relative energy cost per (densely spaced) occupant, building systems longevity, occupant comfort, health and productivity, and the impacts of mixed-use buildings and neighborhoods on the resulting data, the verdict is still out.

The carbon emissions which derive from the operation of buildings, including tall buildings, are said to be over 40 per cent of total emissions from all sources. These emissions are the result of a significant depletion of fossil fuel reserves and materially contribute to the effects of global warming. Energy figures are largely based upon "energy-in-use" accounting and while disturbingly high, generally fail to consider embodied energy costs in the construction of a building, the broader costs of manufacturing energy at its source, or the longer term effects of the building maintenance and operation over time. Simple life-cycle costing techniques on commercial tall buildings are only now being practiced by property managers in an attempt to reduce ongoing costs and increase revenues.

Institutions which commonly occupy tall office buildings often assign great value to the comfort and productivity of their employees. Over the life of an occupancy, staff costs typically range from 85 to 90 per cent of total occupancy costs. What this suggests to an attentive employer is that for a relatively inexpensive upgrade to the environmental well-being and comfort of the working environment (light, air quality, thermal comfort, acoustics, visual field and view), the productivity of staff can be substantially leveraged, given its proportionately high cost to the employer. This fact is seldom identified and understood as a significant opportunity in tall buildings.

Building form, geometry and orientation are among the most important factors in describing a tall building's appetite for energy as well as major cost drivers for each project. With modern parametric design tools, building form can be optimized for structural performance, energy efficiency, spatial and constructibility performance. Orientation can be optimized with regard to climatic conditions such as daylighting, heat gain, aerodynamic effects and the potential for wind harvesting.

The history of the tall building is intrinsically linked to improvements in technology, new materials and innovations in design and construction. Developing technologies in areas such as biomimesis and nanotechnology are yielding more responsive and high-performing materials and systems. Tall buildings provide the opportunity to maximize the economies of scale inherent in monolithic construction projects and processes. Computer-based optimization at many levels, the tendency toward off-site fabrication, under efficient and high-performance conditions, and standardization all bring the potential for energy efficiencies, high quality building systems and longevity to the tall building project.

Finally, the urban context for tall buildings is enormously relevant to the conversation of comprehensive sustainability. The presence of a mixed-use tower, or even a single-use tower in a walkable mixed-use neighborhood, is inevitably tied to the overall energy costs for transportation, recreation, work and residence. Mixed-use buildings can share essential programs, achieve higher levels of utility, better integrate recycling of waste heat and water and reduce peak service loads. Even the parking of cars can be shared and managed more efficiently.

With regard to our topic, in *PERFORMATIVE ECOLOGIES*, we have organized our material around design strategies which attend to the conservation of specific natural resources. Because we are interested in the generally explicit display of these strategies and their prospects for creating new formal languages in architecture, we are taking a case study approach. While some of the projects showcased are illustrative proposals, others are actual projects which have not yet been built. Others are completed and occupied projects with, in some cases, a track record of performance and adaptability.

Briefly, we will review current developments in biomimetic envelopes which act to modulate the effects of the sun (heat, glare, daylighting), and in some cases, natural ventilation, view and privacy. We will then evaluate insular walls which have depth and create 3-dimensional opportunities for greater environmental modulation between interior and exterior conditions. A review of the effects of wind on tall buildings follows with a focus on strategies for wind harvesting and energy conversion. Finally, we will discuss the emerging interest in biological towers, tall buildings that incorporate flora, even urban agriculture, in their programmatic and formal strategies within the context of more holistic urban living.

National Library of France, Paris, 1996 / Dominique Perrault / DPA

Arab World Institute, Paris, 1987 / Jean Nouvel, Gilbert Lézénès, Pierre Soria, Architecture Studio

Solar Heat and Glare

In 1980, eighteen Arab countries agreed to establish the Arab World Institute in Paris. Sited on the left bank of the River Seine in the 5th Arrondissement, the design competition for the building was won by Jean Nouvel, widely known for unique building surfaces and materials. As a visual reference to the traditional Arabic "mashrabiya," Nouvel devised a lattice-like facade of movable diaphragms linked to photosensitive mechanical devices which opened and closed according to the amount of sunlight falling on the building surfaces. These diaphragms, which now no longer work, created the first organic and photo-responsive wall controlling the amount of sunlight and solar heat entering the building. While Paris is not climatically known for solar heat or glare, the Arab World Institute in 1987 became an early pioneer in both the design of biomimetic building facades as well as the explicit integration of such a system into the building's architecture.

Two years later at the National Library of France, also in Paris, Dominique Perrault experimented with complex and layered building skins in an attempt to modify solar conditions. One of Francois Mitterand's "Grand Projects," Perrault designed four 24 story towers, all surrounding a large forested garden. Built to accommodate some 13 million books, the architect sheathed the towers in floor to ceiling glass to maximize the amount of sunlight entering the stacks and reading rooms. In an attempt to control seasonal light quantities and personalize light control, tall interior wood shutters were designed inside the glass skin to regulate light and heat. The overriding architectonic

SailTower, Jeddah, Proposed Completion 2015 / Perkins + Will

GSW Headquarters, Berlin, 1999 / Sauerbruch Hutton

effect of this enormous project was to contrast the infinitely repetitious rectangular glass wall with the inevitable randomness of the shutters within.

Several years later, as Berlin began to rebuild its urban architecture following the unification of East and West Germany, Sauerbruch Hutton added a new office tower to the existing GSW Headquarters. Completed in 1999, the 22-story structure featured a double thermal skin on east and west elevations with operable windows. With a building width limited to 11 meters, natural cross ventilation reduced mechanical ventilation loads by as much as 70 per cent. An interstitial exterior wall depth of almost a meter was fitted with colored perforated aluminum louvers which could be both automatically and manually deployed. These louvers regulated the amount of direct solar radiation and heat entering the broad sides of the office tower. Once again, the variability of these deployable colored screens animated an otherwise gridded and highly repetitive window wall. Also, like Paris' National Library, the manual interface provided visual traces of the human activity within. SailTower by Robert Goodwin of Perkins + Will located in Jeddah, Saudi Arabia employs external shade sails which, when combined with balconies of greater depth, preserve views while providing shade and privacy from adjacent residential suites. This increased depth toward the top of the tower plus the varying orientation of the sails creates a strong visual pattern in the exterior architecture.

These opportunities for personal interface with the environmental elements of a window wall are becoming common

Next Human Network (NHN) Headquarters, Bundang, 2010 / NBBJ

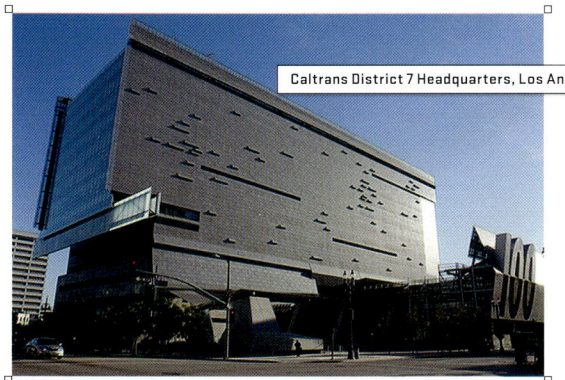

Caltrans District 7 Headquarters, Los Angeles, 2004 / Morphosis

41 Cooper Square, New York City, 2009 / Morphosis

with a range of technologies and architectural outcomes. For the Next Human Network (NHN) headquarters tower in Bundang, Korea by NBBJ and Samoo Architects & Engineers, tall bright green panels, functionally not unlike the Library, line the interior of the floor-to-ceiling window wall. Computer programming activities inside the building require control of natural light and glare and programmers can manually adjust the panels to suit their individual needs.

Since these early experiments in adjustable window walls, others have followed. Morphosis' 2004 Caltrans District 7 Headquarters in downtown Los Angeles was designed as a large government office building whose long elevations were required to orient east and west. In the face of extreme solar exposures, the architects designed a rain-screen exterior wall system of perforated stainless steel panels which were operable at the window lines. These panels were mechanically automated based upon time of day and position of the sun. On the south elevation, the entire window wall is shaded with fixed horizontal sun-screens which are embedded with photo-voltaic cells for the generation of building energy.

Five years later at New York City's 41 Cooper Square, Morphosis took the idea of separate skins, this time an aluminum and glass window-wall system draped on the outside with a matrix of perforated stainless steel panels, highly shaped and expressive. The normative window wall on the interior maximizes natural light coming into the academic spaces and seals the building by conventional means while the exterior "drape" shades the glass during the summer months, allows visibility and provides a canvas for a wide range of compositional gestures which

Hegau Tower, Singen, 2008 / JAHN

Thom Mayne refers to as "contextual." Incorporating similar features, yet pursuing restraint and a kind of formal elegance, Helmut Jahn has completed the Hegau Tower in Singen, Germany. Huge panes of glass and a minimized floor/ceiling spandrel maximizes visibility and natural light. On the long southwestern facade, however, vertical rails guide automated stainless steel louvers down from the window head to the sill, reducing solar heat and glare when called upon. Hopper sashes in the window wall provide natural ventilation.

Functionally equivalent, yet quite the opposite in formal terms, Shigeru Ban has resurrected the roll-down metal shutter familiar to every ground level retail store and European hotel and created the Metal Shutter Houses, a residential building in Manhattan's Chelsea District. Mechanized shutters on the exterior of the building and facing exterior terraces can be opened or closed by the occupants, allowing for open air and full sun or privacy, acoustical insulation and weather protection. As he has been known to do, Ban has recycled a common idea for a new use and allowed the architecture to be the outcome of its purpose.

More extreme skin solutions applied to vertical buildings range from low cost speculative structures to ones which are institutional and highly capitalized. As part of a formerly decrepit industrial zone, the 22@Barcelona, city authorities in Barcelona have targeted sites for new energy-efficient buildings and mixed-use neighborhoods. Media-TIC, a new 10 story speculative media and services office building has been designed by local firm, Cloud 9, to be energy self-sufficient and to reduce carbon emissions by 95 per cent. The building's

PG_35_PERFORMATIVE ECOLOGIES.

Metal Shutter Houses, New York City, 2011 / Shigeru Ban Architects

Media-TIC, Barcelona, 2007 / Enric Ruiz-Geli, Cloud 9

Al Bahr ADIC Towers, Abu Dhabi, 2012 / Aedas

structure is a simple column-free concrete frame wrapped in highly responsive skins, varying according to orientation. The northeast and northwest sides are designed in clear glass while the southeast facade is covered in silk-screened ETFE pillows, equipped with heat sensors that can prompt computer-controlled air pumps which inflate and deflate the three layers of each pillow. The southwest facade is covered in vertical ETFE pillows which are inflated with nitrogen-based gas to filter glare and protect against solar heat gain.

While the Barcelona solution is simply engineered and produced on a minimum budget, the Al Bahr Towers in the center of Abu Dhabi's downtown are highly mechanized and built in the monumental materials one would expect of two 25-story institutional office buildings. Designed by the London offices of Aedas and Arup, the towers form the headquarters for the Abu Dhabi Investment Council (ADIC), the Emirate's primary investment agency. Abu Dhabi's Urban Planning Council (UPC) has targeted high levels of sustainability and incorporated them within the current Plan Abu Dhabi 2030. In the context of the extreme Gulf climate, it was clear to the designers that the most significant measure they could take would be to protect the buildings from direct sunlight. At the same time, highly reflective or dark glass was rejected for the significant reduction of natural light that would result and the corresponding need for energy required for artificial light. Since permanent shading would compromise visibility, a state-of-the-art operable skin was developed to shade the glass in times of direct sun. This "dynamic mashrabiya" acts as solar "flowers" which open and close depending on the position of the sun. Each tower's 2000

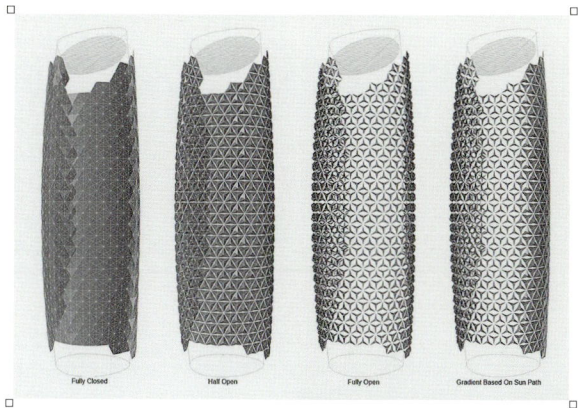

shading units are constructed from 15 components that form a triangular, Teflon-coated fiberglass mesh set in an aluminum and stainless steel frame. These frames are mounted on the exterior of the window walls in the areas of maximum solar radiation and are activated by photo-sensors.

An even more subtle biomimetic skin for architectural applications is being developed from preliminary research done in the field of thermobimetal (TBM) surfaces. Thermobimetals have been used for years in industrial applications wherein two metals are laminated together with different thermal expansion coefficients, resulting in deformations under heating or cooling. As the temperature changes, one side of a laminated sheet will expand or contract at a different rate than the other, resulting in a curved or curled section. In the case of buildings, these reactions to solar radiation or ambient temperatures can result in openings which affect shading and the prospect for natural ventilation (intake or exhaust). Available as strips, disks or spirals, these materials have historically been used in thermostats and other electrical control devices.

In architectural applications, these systems are most akin to the morphogenesis of biological materials wherein form and performance are functionally linked. Michael Weinstock aptly describes this interdependence: "Biological organisms have evolved multiple variations of form that should not be thought of as separate from their structure and materials. Such a distinction is artificial, in view of the complex hierarchies within natural structures and the emergent properties of assemblies. Form, structure and material act upon each other, and this behavior of all three cannot be predicted by

Bloom, Los Angeles, 2011 / DO|SU Studio Architecture

analysis of any one of them separately."[5]

In the Bloom project, a 20 foot tall shade canopy designed by Doris Sung, Ingalill Wahlroos-Ritter and Matthew Melnyk, the surface is populated with metal flaps shaped to capture the sun's rays throughout the day. With the use of digital analysis, the size of the flaps and openings are optimized to shade and ventilate the area beneath the structure. In order to create the thinnest possible shell, lightweight structural framing is incorporated directly into the shell, creating a monocoque skin assembly. As a result and in the form of a multifunctional skin, a bio-responsive system both shades the interior as well as ventilates it. Much research in these technologies is underway with the prospect of achieving widespread architectural application one day.

Architectural Insulation

Perhaps no one has made double-skin window walls more fully-integrated or fashionable than Christoph Ingenhoven, the energy-conscious architect from Dusseldorf, Germany. With his early headquarters office tower for RWE in Essen (1996), he displayed the numerous insular advantages of the "double-skin activated facade." This system is generally comprised of two layers of glass, separated by an interstitial layer of air, of which the outer layer insulates against noise, wind and temperature change. The air space between the two provides natural ventilation. Sun shading and glare control can be built inside the facade or in the interstitial layer with, for example internal blinds which also control solar heat gain to the interior of the building.

1 Bligh Office Tower, Sydney, 2011 / Ingenhoven Architects

Ingenhoven's firm has completed eight buildings around the world which employ double-skin facades. He believes that while the more northerly a project is located, the more effective the system is, double skins can also be effective in equatorial regions. The key to achieving energy savings is the extent of the interstitial layer of air: the greater the volume in the cavity, the more effective the system. Double-skin systems are considerably more expensive than single-skins and have typically been used throughout Europe and Japan with fewer employed in the US due to historically lax energy regulation and the predominant development focus on initial versus life-cycle costs.

The firm's most iconic example of these layered systems is 1 Bligh Office Tower in Sydney, Australia, a more recent relative of the earlier RWE headquarters in Essen. The radial office tower has a fluid shape which allows wind velocities to accelerate along the exterior glass line. The double-skin system in place here is 35 inches in depth and naturally ventilates each floor at its level. The inner skin is high-performance coated glass while the outer skin is clear glass. In order to reduce the depths of the floor and maximize the impact of natural light, the interior of the building has a vertical atrium which brings additional light and natural ventilation into the center of the office space.

SOM's recent Jinao Tower in Nanjing, China looks to integrate multiple systems into a double-skin cavity wall system. At 56 stories, the tower requires significant structural shear resistance. With a need to puncture the circulation core at the center of the building, an exterior braced frame was developed to lighten the burden of the core. In a

RWE Headquarters, Essen, 1997 / Ingenhoven Architects

collaboration of structural engineering, architecture and environmental engineering, a diagonalized steel braced frame was designed which when paired with the same on the opposite side of the building comprises a full X brace. This brace is held away from the concrete frame sufficiently to provide a ventilated cavity and a fractal pattern which forms the architecture of the building. Wind studies indicate that slots on the windward side of the building accept air into the cavity and force air out horizontally at the leeward side. This flushing provides natural ventilation and constitutes high-performance insulation during both the hot summer and the cool winter months. During the summer, the ventilation allows the hot air to be extracted from the cavity while during the winter, built-up heat in the cavity can be used to maintain the heat within the building. The ultimate effect of this strategy has been to reduce the demands on the base building mechanical systems by up to 20 per cent.

Manitoba Hydro Place is the headquarters tower for Manitoba Hydro, the major electric and natural gas utility in the Province of Manitoba. The building is located in Winnipeg, known for extreme winter and summer temperatures. Designed by Kuwabara Payne McKenna Blumberg Architects and assisted by Transsolar, the building maximizes passive solar, wind and geothermal energy. Climate studies indicate that although winter temperatures can be well below zero for days on end, the skies are frequently sunny, thereby delivering significant solar energy.

While appearing as a single 18 story tower, Manitoba Hydro Place is actually two towers which intersect at the northern end of the site at a solar chimney. The chimney draws air out of the

Manitoba Hydro, Manitoba, 2009 / KPMB

Macquarie Apartments Aurora Place, Sydney, 2000 / Renzo Piano Building Workshop

building during the warmer months and in winter, exhaust air is drawn to the bottom of the chimney by fans where heat is recovered and used to preheat incoming cold air. At the other end, the towers splay to reveal three south facing 6 story atria. With Winnipeg's characteristic southerly wind and its sunny skies, these glass atria collect solar heat to augment winter heating and, through a louver system in the glass wall, naturally ventilate during the summer. At the long glass elevations of the building, a double-skin system combines manually operated windows in the interior curtain wall combined with automated exterior wall vents controlled by the building management. In this way, employees can affect their own comfort while management oversees overall building efficiency and operations.

By the end of the 1990s, these various double-skin cavity systems began to be explored for their spatial possibilities. Renzo Piano's Macquarie Apartments in Sydney, Australia's Aurora Place occupy the insulating layer at the perimeter of that building. At the apartment tower which has expansive views of the Sydney Harbor, Piano arranged deep balconies along the perimeter and fully glazed them. Through a combination of glass balustrades, structural glass louvers and metal blinds, Piano recreated the multiple window coverings (drape, window, shutter) familiar to many Europeans living in historic housing. Within the context of a highly tectonic exterior wall, a resident can close the glass louvers and insulate his/her interior from the cold exterior, or activate the blinds to eliminate light and noise or open everything including the glass louvers to naturally ventilate either the balcony or the entire living unit. These kinds of opportunities suggest greater permeability and spatial possibility

Shanghai Tower Skygarden Section, Shanghai, 2014 / Gensler

at the point where the building interior meets the exterior. Perhaps the most elaborate double-skin tower, and proposed to be the world's second tallest building, will be the Shanghai Tower project, designed by Gensler for the Lujiazui district in Pudong. At 121 stories, the building is vertically organized into 12 to 15 story segments, comprising different occupancies and publicly accessible perimeter atria between the interior and exterior skins. As these exterior gardens are accessible only at the bottom of each atrium, it is only necessary to provide chilled and heated air at the lower register of each. The rest of the volume will be ventilated by way of a natural updraft. The tortile shape of the tower was devised, through wind tunnel testing, to resist typhoons and reduce loading from wind vortices by some 24 per cent. There is little question that, assuming a need for such a tall building, the swirling exterior creates the opportunity to both insulate the body of the building and capture open space at its perimeter. The quality of interior design and programming of these spaces will indicate whether these atria will be richly differentiated as well as become meaningful extensions of the adjacent space in the tower's core.

Finally, a competition entry by the New York office of Perkins + Will for the Al-Birr Foundation Headquarters in Riyadh, Saudi Arabia suggests a more radical version of the double-skin tower. Attempting to take inspiration from the Muslim elements of the spiral minaret, the walled garden and the "mashrabiya," the architects have resisted the aggressive shape-making which characterizes tall buildings in the Gulf region. A simple rectangular shape on the exterior, presumably framed and skinned in glass, surrounds

Al-Birr Foundation Headquarters, Riyadh / Perkins + Will

another shape which includes a ground level atrium, an ascending mass and roof-top gardens with plantings and privileged views. The more complex shape within retains its own skin which suggests insulation, the possibility for sun control, natural ventilation, and the freedom of designing floors to a more specific set of programs. Additionally, this dichotomy may offer a solution to the desire to mediate the necessary individuality of each tower's program with the urban design preference of building out the street and providing a level of consistency to the public domain.

Capturing Solar Energy

Photovoltaic cell (PVC) technology has been widely available to buildings for over ten years now and yet struggles to gain universal traction. Many reasons exist for this, among them, worldwide shortages of silicon keep prices high. Also, the enormous global market share which China has come to control has resulted in failures within the US domestic industry. A number of "thin film" installations have failed, sewing seeds of doubt in the marketplace while an inability to integrate cell technology into conventional and widely applicable building products persists. Stand-alone photovoltaic panels atop roofs and parking structures are common but the integration of PVCs into glass window-wall systems or insulated cladding and rain-screens has been slow. Few large scale building projects are willing to risk untested new products without a track record and service data. Finally, there exists a perception in the building industry that while PVC arrays are visible and generate good will, their

Heron Tower, Bishopsgate, London, 2011 / KPF

actual impact on total energy consumption on a large, or tall, building is small. However, the 46-story Heron Tower in London's Bishopsgate was designed by the London offices of Kohn Pederson Fox and Arup. Completed in 2011 and now the city's second tallest building, the tower is notable for its unique floor plan organization and its major commitment to building-integrated photovoltaics (BIPV). Contrary to conventional tall office buildings which have centralized cores doing multiple duty for vertical circulation, utilities and structural bracing, Heron has a side-loaded core which leaves the floor unobstructed for greater space-planning flexibility and unimpeded views of London. With the elevators, utilities and fire exits abutting the south side of the plan, constituting a kind of opacity to the southern rotation of the sun, the designers state that they have created a "solar shield" against radiation to the building interior.

As a result, they have chosen to integrate 3,000 square meters of photovoltaic arrays into the south elevation of the building, reducing solar gain and generating an estimated 92 megawatts of electricity per year. The power this generates meets 2.5 per cent of the building's electricity demand, reducing its carbon emissions by 850,000 kilograms a year. The PVCs are supplied by Q Cells of Germany, laminated between glass panels by sub-contractor, Scheuten Glass, and installed directly into the curtain-wall. What is unique here is the successful large-scale integration of the work of architects, engineers, manufacturers, installers and building contractor into an effective building product.

Federation of Korean Industries Tower, Seoul, 2013 / Adrian Smith + Gordon Gill

In the case of the Federation of Korean Industries Tower under construction in Seoul and designed by Adrian Smith and Gordon Gill, BIPVs have altered the shape and surface of the architecture. At over 800 feet in height, the building concept is simple: a rectangular office building with a central core and several multi-story atria within the body of the tower and at its various corners. Photovoltaic panels have been integrated into the spandrel and window wall system with the spandrel sloped back at 30 degrees to maximize the collection of solar radiation. Beneath the spandrel, the high performance vision glass is sloped forward to shade and minimize the amount of radiation entering the building interior. This manipulation of the curtain wall creates a horizontally "pleated" effect which the architects have limited to the southwest and northwest elevations where the low afternoon sun provides maximum solar impact.

Due to current energy policies in South Korea and a renewable tax credit system, building developers are able to collect subsidies for the electricity they sell back to the grid at a rate of seven times that of the electricity they purchase. This subsidy runs up to a certain limit and the architects state that integrating solar collection into the two building elevations equates to that limit. The Seoul tower efficiently captures the maximum energy subsidy available and creates a distinctive surface architecture through its straightforward response to the requirements of solar technology. Appropriate energy policy appears to be key to incentivizing opportunity.

Contrary to popular belief, light levels in the UK and

Northern Europe are generally sufficient to make PVCs viable, with photovoltaic cells generating power even on cloudy days. The Cooperative Insurance Society (CIS) Tower in Manchester was built in 1962 and after forty years, was experiencing failure of its windowless, mosaic-tiled facade. Committed to a green strategy, the building owners teamed with Solarcentury in 2006 to reclad the entire building, in the process, developing and installing 7,244 80 watt fully-integrated photovoltaic panels on the east, south and west elevations. These panels provide complete waterproofing and exterior finish for the tower and make the retrofit project the largest building solar array in Europe.

Another, if seldom-used, device for exploiting the sun's rays is a heliostat, a mirror array which tracks the sun's movements and then, by way of preprogrammed sequencing directions from software or by responding to exterior sensors, sunlight can be directed to needed locations. Occasionally, these heliostats are part of a more complex system of lenses and fiber-optic cables which capture sunlight and direct light through more intricate pathways.

In New York's Battery Park City, Michael Van Valkenburgh's outdoor garden, Teardrop Park South, has been illuminated by an array of 3 heliostats mounted atop the Verdesian, an adjacent 23 story residential tower. The park is located at the base of the U-shaped Riverhouse and receives no sunlight for many months. James Carpenter and Davidson Norris of New York's Carpenter Norris Consulting have devised the plan and designed the 8 foot diameter heliostats to reflect oval beams of sunlight onto particular benches and trees within the park. While the system captures and redirects solar energy in useful ways, it does not raise the ambient light levels in the park. Much research and experimentation is currently underway in Europe, however, to create more adaptable systems and products to accomplish this.

Wind and Natural Ventilation

While short buildings may have little interaction with wind and the pressures it can induce, tall buildings are generally exposed to significant wind forces and must be designed to counteract them and minimize the collateral effects wind can cause. Think of a tall building as a very large sail on a sail boat and you begin to envision the effects of wind and the stresses it can induce. As buildings grow taller than 20 to 30 stories, lateral forces (wind and earthquakes), as opposed to gravity loads, become the dominant factors in their structural design.

Conventional rectangular tall buildings are generally sited such that at least one of their tall flat walls is in the direction of the oncoming wind. As the wind diverts around the building, it creates eddies at the vertical corners which can "pull" on the building, rather than "push" on it. Additionally, at certain velocities and in response to certain gusts, severe transverse wind pressures can appear on the two sides of such a building. This creates irregular lateral forces acting on the tower. Frequently, this activity generates down drafts as well which accelerate surface wind velocity to the base of the building.

From a design perspective, buildings can be designed to be aerodynamic. Fluid, smoother shapes which allow the wind to pass with less impact are now more frequently conceived and tall buildings can be oriented with their long axis in the direction of the prevailing wind rather than transverse to it. Occasionally, altering the surface of a tall building with steps or balconies can reduce wind loads. Buildings which bulge or are tortile over the length of their shafts can interrupt the down drafts and reduce wind disturbance at the base. The design of tall buildings to minimize wind-induced stresses reduces not only the weight of the structural frame but the curtain wall assembly, the anchorage and glazing systems as well. This results in a more efficient and less costly building. While municipal codes typically address wind loading, both an area's unique climatic character as well as a tall building's particular profile and surface characteristics are cause for wind tunnel testing which is a standard procedure for quantifying wind impacts on tall building designs.

Norman Foster's Swiss Re Tower at 30 St. Mary Axe in London, otherwise known as the "gherkin," was expressly designed to neutralize wind pressure variations on the building and to foil down drafts which would affect the comfort of its street-level plaza and entry. Automated triangular

The Cooperative Insurance Society (CIS), Manchester 1962 / Solarcentury

30 St Mary Axe "Gherkin", London, 2003 / Foster + Partners

KfW Westarkade, Frankfurt, 2010 / Sauerbruch Hutton

"flaps" act as operable windows to draw air into the stacked series of atria which surround the building. Their operation is further calibrated to respond to available ventilation and wind speed.

One of the most remarkable new tall buildings, and winner of the World's Best Tall Building for 2011 by the Council on Tall Buildings and Urban Habitat, is the KfW Westarkade building in Frankfurt. This tower of modest height employs a highly integrated window wall which exploits wind and natural ventilation to an advanced degree. Berlin's Sauerbruch Hutton designed the building for one of Germany's major banks, KfW, which funds many of Germany's ambitious energy-conservation programs.

The 10 story tower has a flowing form which responds to the prevailing wind direction and consists of a sawtooth-shaped window wall which captures the wind for natural ventilation. Inside the wall is a cavity as deep as 28 inches which encloses automated blinds to control solar gain and glare. The exterior window is comprised of fixed tempered glass panes while the interior glazing is operable. At the exterior return are colorful ventilation flaps which are controlled by a roof-mounted weather station that monitors wind speed and direction and controls the flaps. The cavities fill with air and then enter the interior office space by way of the operable windows and/or vents at the perimeter of each floor. The air is ultimately exhausted through the negatively-pressurized corridors at the building core.

In Dubai, the Burj Al-Taqa, otherwise known as the Dubai Energy Tower, designed by Eckhard Gerber, is a 68-story tower with a straightforward approach to using wind as

Strata SE1, London, 2010 /BFLS

Bahrain World Trade Center, Bahrain, 2008 / Atkins

a passive resource. While its menu of green strategies is broad, the building attempts to create a modern version of a "badgir," a wind tower traditionally built by wealthy Iranians. Historically, these towers drew in cool air high which then sank to the ground forcing the hot air to the ceiling where it was naturally exhausted. With a similar convection system, air is brought in at the base of the tower and vertically travels to exhaust systems at the roof. At the roof level, a 200 foot wind turbine crowns the tower and generates electrical energy for the building. The goal of the building is to be energy self-sufficient.

Another tall building with explicit wind turbine technology is central London's Strata SE1, a residential tower designed as a catalyst for redevelopment in the Elephant & Castle neighborhood. The radial walls of the apartment tower neutralize irregular wind pressures on the skin and the building top is cut away to reveal three nine meter five blade wind turbines. The wind at the top of the tower is accelerated through these three openings and power a turbine which is projected to supply over 8 per cent of the building's electrical energy requirements.

Wind turbine technology is beginning to appear regularly in tall building literature, in experimental proposals, and, occasionally, in actual building construction. For the Bahrain World Trade Center Tower designed by Atkins, two sail-shaped towers have been designed to curve into the void between the two, accelerating wind into three bridges which each carry one large 29 meter wind turbine. The shape of the towers as well as the location of large propellers are an explicit response to wind power with a goal

COR Tower, Miami / Oppenheim Architecture+Design

Pearl River Tower, Guangzhou, 2013 /SOM

of 1100 megawatts of power per year. The Dubai International Financial Centre Lighthouse Tower, also by Atkins, employs the traditional "mashrabiya" screen as a compositional skin element which clads the bulk of the tower and then breaks free at the top to contain three large wind turbines which yaw in order to maximize the impact of incoming wind velocity. Oppenheim Architecture + Design's plans for Miami's COR Tower include a simple rectangular shape enclosing a mix of residential, office and retail uses. The unique architectural features of the tower are the large round windows which, at the top of the building, rise above the roof level to contain wind propellers and turbines framed on the skyline of Miami.

A series of three buildings by Adrian Smith and Gordon Gill, one while they were with Skidmore, Owings & Merrill, displays a different attitude about smooth building form, aerodynamics and wind capture. The 71-story Pearl River Tower in Guangzhou, China for the Guangdong Tobacco Company is an aerodynamically advanced building mass which neutralizes eccentric wind pressures while establishing its own architectural language. The building in plan is curved to capture and direct wind into the center of the tower. At two intermediate mechanical floors, the skin recesses to receive accelerated wind into a system of wind turbines. This initial design set the stage for subsequent wind-conscious towers such as the Wuhan Greenland Center in Wuhan, China at the confluence of the Yangtze and Han rivers. Similarly, Smith + Gill's proposal for the Clean Technology Tower, designed as a net-zero-energy prototype, retains both the earlier aerodynamic forms and the integration of turbines at the corners of the tower where the wind vortices collect.

Wuhan Greenland Center, Wuhan, Planned Completion 2017 / Adrian Smith + Gordon Gill

Vertical Flora

The great challenge ahead for the integration of biological systems into the tall building form is nowhere better epitomized than in the architecture of Ken Yeang. Yeang, a Malaysian architect, trained in England and practicing throughout South Asia since his return in 1976, has always focused on what he calls "bioclimatic design" as a strategy for creating environmentally responsive tall buildings. More recently, he has referred to "ecomimesis" as a way to envision a tall building functioning as nature does.

Yeang's career began with a series of houses, most notably his own, the "Roof-Roof House," in which many of his later ideas for tall buildings can be seen in incipient form. A free-floating canopy throws shade on the building below, deep balconies capture breezes and provide for outdoor living while shading walls and openings below. Windows are set deep into the exterior wall to keep them protected from the sun. Landscape occurs at both the ground plane as well as on the many upper terraces of the house.

Beginning in the mid-1980s and into the 1990s, Yeang designed and built a number of tall buildings in South Asia. Many of these failed to gain broad attention, however, they displayed his persistence in attempting to create an environmental tall building and bringing plant material above the ground plane and into the building's vertical architecture. The most architecturally compelling of the built work remains the Menara Mesiniaga, a small and eccentric office tower completed in 1992. Located on the outskirts of Kuala Lumpur, this 15 story office building for a local IBM franchise stands somewhat apart from the rest of his built work in its more complete integration of the environmental tools with which Yeang had been working. At the same time, the building is highly erratic, employing an array of architectural treatments that makes it look like an experiment of sorts. Its aspirational tone is touching and likeable and viewed now from a distance of two decades, his work exhibits the difficulty the building industry has had in absorbing the lessons of truly green architecture.

In Menara Mesiniaga, various wall systems are suspended from a structural frame and depending upon solar orientation, are varied to protect the interior space from solar heat gain. The glass curtain-wall is recessed inside the frame and tinted to provide additional shade to the interior. Episodic cavities in the mass exist to create balconies and terraces and a skeletal framework exists at the top of the building as if it were awaiting plants, telecommunications equipment or commercial advertising. The ground plane slopes up to the second and third floors bringing plant materials up into the base of the tower. The building has a quirky and futuristic Bucky Fuller-meets-Archigram quality about it. While he has continued to publicize his ideas profusely, teach and lecture widely, and has created countless proposals for tall buildings worldwide, his work largely remains a part of the theoretical critique of "bioclimatic design" rather than the legacy of built environmental skyscrapers.

The gulf which exists between a comprehensive critique of bioclimatic design and its actual integration into the tall building form, as epitomized by Yeang's work, is real. Designs exist for strategies which are focused and seem implementable such as Édouard François' Vegetation Tower for Nantes, France while others are highly conceptual and futuristic such as Ma Yansong's Floating Island Over the Central Business District of Beijing. Both kinds of projects assume their positions in the archives of professional conversation about bringing natural systems to the urban environment and the aspiration for uniting built form and nature. Neither will be built.

One of the most recent bioclimatic projects to be built which allows us to gage the realm of the possible is the SIEEB Sino-Italian Ecological and Energy Efficient Building for Tsinghua University in Beijing designed by Mario Cucinella Architects. A joint development of Tsinghua and the Polytechnic University of Milan, the building's program is to research building efficiencies and environmental compatibility. As such, the building envelope is, among its other qualities, an explicit response to solar orientation. A simple U-shape in plan, the building's north facade contains unprotected glazed openings. On the east and west sides, openings are protected by a double wall system which both shades and naturally ventilates its own vertical plenum. On the south side, the building steps back floor by floor, producing generous outdoor terraces which are protected by deeply framed cantilevers containing photovoltaic arrays, shading the full expanses of floor to ceiling windows and creating opportunities for abundant planting. At the base of the building, a ground level and basement grotto runs the

EDITT Tower, Singapore / Ken Yeang / T. R. Hamzah & Yeang

Planted Tower of Nantes, Nantes / Maison Édouard François

Menara Mesiniaga, Subang Jaya, Selangor, 1992 / Ken Yeang / T. R. Hamzah & Yeang

SIEEB Sino-Italian and Energy Efficient Building, Tsinghua University, Beijing 2006 / Mario Cucinella

length of the site bringing water and plant material through the entire project.

Another aspect of vertical flora for which there is much current research and exploration is the prospect of vertical farming. As compelling as these farms are from a macro-cultural perspective, there are far more proposals and experiments today than examples of built work. The majority of this area of study is based upon the economics of food production, trends in demographics and a concern, ultimately, for sustainable environmental practices.

The central premise for this topic is an acknowledgement that more than 50 per cent of the world's population now dwell in urban centers. By the year, 2050, projections suggest that the earth's population will grow by over 3 billion persons, to nearly 9 billion, and, by that time, 80 per cent will reside in cities. In order to feed that population, extrapolating current data, we will require 109 million additional hectares of farmland, equal to the land mass of Brazil.

Today's 800 million hectares of soil-based agriculture represents 38 per cent of the earth's total land mass and plant cultivation has been growing at the expense of natural ecosystems. New health hazards have arisen due to the creation of ecotones, regions where cultivation has encroached and modified natural ecologies, bringing infectious disease agents into the agricultural and human interface. The response of industrial farming has been to combat these agents through a toxic mix of pesticides and fungicides. These elements create further health hazards to our soil, aquifers and, ultimately, to our food supply.

Creating efficient vertical farms within the city offers many distinct advantages over current methods. Among them: crop production can operate year-round without the threat of weather-related failures and the agricultural run-off and chemical pollution endemic to soil-based farming can be eliminated. One could expect a reduction in fossil fuel use as crop transport and farm equipment would be significantly curtailed. Through high-level filtration, municipal waste could be recycled from black water to gray water for irrigation to, ultimately, drinking water, all within the city. The risk of disease transmission from natural to agricultural systems would be significantly reduced and farmlands would be returned to nature, restoring damaged ecosystems and forests, playing a significant role in carbon sequestration and the reversal of global climate change. Finally, a culture of agricultural employment and healthy food within the city would likely be a positive cultural trend.

Indoor farming is, of course, not a new phenomenon. Greenhouse-based agriculture has been in existence for decades. Many crops have been sold commercially and worldwide such as strawberries, tomatoes, peppers, cucumbers and herbs. Certain freshwater fishes, crustaceans and mollusks have also been farmed indoors. What is being proposed now by specialists, such as Dr. Dickson Despommier of Columbia University's Department of Environmental Health Sciences, is the creation of vertical buildings which would support hydroponic, aeroponic and similarly efficient greenhouse agriculture. Within an urban policy framework which would eliminate vacant lots and underutilized sites, tall buildings could be erected to create a locavore culture in which planting, husbandry, harvest and food delivery would all happen within the domain of the city. Estimates have been made that a standard city block with a 30 story farm (3 million square feet) could produce enough food (2,000 calories/person) for up to 50,000 people. While more and more city-dwellers independently build small food gardens on rooftops and decks, the necessary support for large-scale applications has not yet materialized.

[3] Giedion, Sigfried, *Mechanization Takes Command*. 1st Edition ed. op. cit.
[4] Banham, Reyner, *Architecture of the Well-Tempered Environment*. Second Edition ed, op. cit.
[5] Weinstock, Michael, *Self Organization and Material Constructions*, Architectural Design Mar.-Apr. 2006, op. cit., 34.

CHAPTER TWO

PERFORMATIVE SKINS

Crystal Palace, London, 1851 / Joseph Paxton

Glass Skyscraper, Berlin, 1922 / Ludwig Mies van der Rohe

Bauhaus Building, Dessau, 1926 / Walter Gropius

The historical roots of today's curtain wall systems can be found in the great 19th century iron and glass greenhouse structures built in the United Kingdom and Europe. Large glass conservatories and nurseries were common in the more established public gardens and private estates. London's Crystal Palace of 1851 designed by the engineer, Joseph Paxton, exhibited to the public the breathtaking architectural possibilities of assembling wrought and cast iron structural members with a growing and increasingly affordable supply of flat industrial glass. While the conventional approach to building taller buildings continued to rely on thick, load-bearing masonry walls, over time and into the early 20th century, this early model of isolating the structural frame from the skin and maximizing the transparency of that skin with improved technologies for glass and support systems became predominant.

Curiously, while frame and curtain wall systems became more visible and offered the benefits of lighter, faster and less expensive construction, the initial tendency on the part of architects was to revert to the aesthetics of Beaux Arts masonry construction for buildings which had already been technically transformed. In Chicago, Daniel Burnham's Reliance Building of 1894, and the Gage Building of 1898 by Holabird & Roche with Louis Sullivan were examples of this early trend. As early Modernism evolved, an emphasis on expressive functionality and an architectural interest in the products of the emerging industrial culture emerged. Visions, if only proposals, for tall buildings, particularly in Europe, began to exploit the imagery of an articulated frame and curtain-wall typology more explicitly. Both of Mies van der Rohe's 1921 and 1922 proposals for skyscrapers in Berlin clearly depicted all-glass skins draped over interior systems of structural columns, slabs and central cores. Walter Gropius' 1926 Bauhaus Building in Dessau contained broad multi-story elevations of an all-glass curtain wall while Le Corbusier's many images of a modernized Paris throughout the 20s always depicted glass curtain wall towers.

By mid-century and in the wake of World War II, the American aluminum industry had advanced in scale and production quality under the pressures of wartime and postwar aircraft production. Because of the excess production capacity available after the war, the cost for finished aluminum was relatively low. The industry developed methods whereby thermoplastic aluminum alloys could be extruded into complex strips and assembled into "sticks," the linear frames which would capture the building glass and attach it to the primary structural frame. Soon thereafter, the invention of the float glass process for manufacturing flat glass overtook the historic production of drawn-glass and this development made glass economically viable. As it happened, this occurred just as the first examples of glass high-rise towers began making their debuts in the mid-1950s and, with considerably greater volume, in the 1960s and beyond. Ultimately, real estate developers began to understand that with the thinner glass curtain walls and within a given building perimeter, they could increase a building's gross leasable area while, at the same time, installing the exterior glass skin at a cost below that of a conventional masonry wall.

In the intervening years, much has changed, both in the expectations of tall building skin technologies and in their ability to perform in a myriad of ways. Marc Schiler says: "Technology suddenly allows us to create truly performative skins. There is an historical confluence of new materials and methods, but also of design, documentation and construction software. We can define a curved or doubly-curved surface and populate it with highly reflective and selective materials. We can make thousands of elements with individual measurements and placements, resulting in perfect geometric forms. Such facades, by their very form and material, bring about certain events. We are able to do things which were impossible. It is a tipping point in construction."[6] This is certainly true in the case of tall buildings where these new capabilities are employed and have long-term impact.

Due to the importance of daylighting and the commercial value assigned to views in tall buildings, glass is by far the predominant material in contemporary skins. Despite its vulnerability in extreme loading conditions (blast and impact) and its generally poor thermal and acoustical performance, glass remains ubiquitous. The American Society of Heating, Refrigerating and Air-Conditioning Engineers (ASHRAE) continues to attempt to limit the extent of glass in building facades as a method for improving energy efficiency, however, the glass industry has been successful in blocking such limitations. The result will likely be a continuation of the extensive use of glass, but glass with higher performance values, whether coated, tinted, screened, insulated, fritted, shaded, or treated with other applications.

The performance requirements of glass have expanded such that a vast array of products and processes have now been engineered even as continued research and development are underway. BIG GLASS: Overseas manufacturers are now capable of producing oversized glass panels (in excess of 45 feet by 10 feet). BENT GLASS: Thermoplastically bent glass is giving way to cold bending during installation or by bending and laminating the glass prior to installation. This process avoids the surface distortions common in heat bending. Geometric complexity in the tall building facade will continue now that parametric modeling tools such as Rhino and Grasshopper are common among students and practitioners. Optimization is a computational process which rationalizes these distorted surfaces and aims to standardize panelization within the overall facade. THIN GLASS: Various one inch assemblies (and larger) exist for curtain walls which sandwich a combination of thermally insulated glass layers and coatings, tints, films and aerogels plus sun control devices within the cavities. DEEP GLASS: Also, deeper interstitial glass walls are emerging which provide for insulation, sun-shading, ventilation, even maintenance and circulation space between exterior wall surfaces. INTEGRATED GLASS describes a wide range of strategies which attempt to incorporate additional functionality into the facade such as sensors, illumination, structure and photovoltaics, to name a few examples.

In PERFORMATIVE SKINS, we consider the primary materials and design strategies currently employed to achieve highly performative exterior walls. Various building projects will be examined as case studies to illustrate the resulting architectural effects. We will conclude with the trend toward informational walls, which is to say, the ability to imbue the skins of tall buildings with informational content by way of electronic media. As in so many other ways, the tall building has, at the current moment, become the intersection point between sudden technological breakthroughs and certain cultural developments, in this case, the continued high valuation assigned to information and the public's familiarity with navigating it.

Glass Technologies

The architectural facade has always been an area of keen interest for architects and building owners. It is generally judged in terms of its performance characteristics and its appearance, and both are now coming under complex scrutiny. Some of this is due to the worldwide attention paid to energy management and rapid climate change. Fluctuations in energy and material prices as well as unpredictable world markets and economic conditions affect design decisions about the ultimate facade selected for each building.

Over the course of the past 20 years, architects have found glass to be an increasingly compelling choice for tall building exteriors. In addition to the ongoing performative advancements of the material which are many, its expanding range of visual properties has attracted architects and engineers for its expressive capabilities. Despite ASHRAE's efforts and energy codes which attempt to restrict the amount of conventional glazing allowed on building facades, the material's reputation for poor thermal and acoustical insulation as well as its inability to resist blast and impact, the use of glass continues to grow. Visibility, the prospect for daylighting and the potential for a wide range of architectural effects appear to be the reasons for this upward trend. While clear plate glass may be on the wane, many other, higher performing glasses are taking its place.

As glass production becomes an expanding global industry, it is now so economically competitive that the industry has redirected its efforts to value-added products which are based upon the production of float glass. Products with performance-enhancing characteristics such as laminated, insulated or coated glass are increasing. Evaluating the aesthetic properties of these glasses is now complex as it involves, at a minimum, color, transparency and reflectivity.

When the sun's rays hit the surface of a glass building, they deliver both heat and light in almost equal parts. To block the heat while allowing the light into the building, high-performance, low-emissivity (low-e) coatings have been developed. Low-e coatings are thin layers of metal applied to the inner surfaces of the glass. These reduce the amount of heat entering a building, thus reducing the cooling loads required to remove the heat. Three metrics are generally used to quantify the performance levels of these glasses.

The Solar Heat Gain Coefficient (SHGC) measures the

portion of directly transmitted and absorbed solar energy entering a building's interior. The lower the SHGC, the higher performing the glass is. This reduction can be affected by using coatings, tints, fritted or silk-screened patterns, embedded shading systems, insulating layers in the glass assembly or combinations of these treatments. U-value is another performance characteristic which measures the heat gain or heat loss through glass due to the differences between indoor and outdoor temperatures. Like SHGC, the lower the U-value, the higher the performance. Finally, Visible Light Transmittance (VLT) is a percentage based upon how much light is transmitted into interior space through the window wall. One hundred per cent is not achievable as that equates to the amount of light passing through an unobstructed opening in a wall. An insulating unit made up of two sheets of clear uncoated glass is approximately 79 per cent. Two misconceptions occur with VLT. One is that providing glass with high VLT is good because it increases daylighting levels. Unfortunately, it also increases glare (relative brightness ratio) which encourages occupants to close the window coverings, waste the solar energy and turn the lights on, requiring electrical energy and additional air changes. The other misconception is that glass with a low VLT is less transparent or harder to see through than glass with a high VLT. Reducing the VLT lowers contrast between the intense sunlight outside and the darker interior. Optically, it does not make the glass harder to see through.

One of the most common glass assemblies employed to reduce energy requirements in a building is insulating glass, the most typical version of which is made from two sheets of glass separated by a hermetically sealed airspace. It is this airspace which provides insulation between the exterior and interior temperatures. When a heat-resistant coating or silk-screen pattern is applied to the assembly, either will function most efficiently when it is applied to the second surface so that incoming heat is stopped before it enters the airspace.

Customized glasses and the custom application of existing glass products are always ongoing. Prismatic, or crystallized, glass is both an existing product and one on which experiments are currently being done. This product is extremely clear with very high transmittance owing to the fact that it contains roughly ten per cent of the iron of normal clear plate glass. As a result, it exhibits none of that glass's green cast and transmits very white light. In certain configurations, it can be used as a prism and will refract incoming white light into arrays of colored light. PPG Starfire glass is one such product as is a new product soon to be introduced by Australia-based Glassform.

One World Trade Center, SOM's tower at Lower Manhattan's Ground Zero, experimented with prismatic glass for its base, however, it failed to meet blast tests and was abandoned for a more conventional treatment. Henning Larsen and Olafur Eliasson's Harpa Concert Hall in Reykjavik is comprised of a range of prismatic glass, reflective glass, colored glass and dichroic glass panels, the latter, reflecting particular light wavelengths which provide color.

Glass interlayers and digital printing is now becoming common. In Europe, David Chipperfield has experimented with SEFAR Architecture Vision and DuPont Sentry Glass interlayer, a new fabric with a translucent single-sided metal coating. As decorative patterns and messaging continues to lure architects, digital printing technologies move from building interiors to the outer skins of major buildings. Los Angeles' Pulp Studio is the only manufacturer of glass building products utilizing Sentry Glass interlayers, marketed in North America as Chromavision. Major American glass producer, Viracon, is marketing a high-definition silkscreen process for architects, allowing them to apply virtually any visual content to a glass window wall.

Architects are asking for larger and larger spans of glass, forcing manufacturers to install larger fabrication equipment. Where 6 feet by 12 feet used to be rule of thumb for architects looking to install large glass panels on a tower facade, General Glass International (GGI) has acquired a furnace which can temper glass up to 110 by 236 inches (over 9 feet by nearly 20 feet). Sheets of glass this large are frequently limited in size not by overall dimension but by deflection resistance, glass thickness or the lamination processes which are necessary to stabilize the glass.

One of the most surprising developments in glass technology is in the category of glass referred to as "smart glass," "switchable glass" or "dynamic glass." These materials are glass units whose opacity or reflectivity can be altered to deflect or transmit more or less of the sun's energy by manipulating electrical currents through the units. A dynamic glass barrier can be optimally tailored to environmental conditions as they vary throughout the day or year. These dynamic glasses have been developed in three technologies: polymer dispersed liquid crystal, suspended particle and electrochromic devices.

While offering no energy-saving benefits, liquid crystal products are comprised of two layers of glass which sandwich transparent electrical conductors enveloping a thin layer of liquid crystal droplets. In the "off" position, the liquid crystals scatter light, giving the unit a milky white appearance, but when an electrical current is applied, the crystals align according to the electrical field and assume a transparent state. The change is instantaneous. Suspended particle glass is similar in its assembly except that microscopic rod-like particles rather than liquid crystals float in a fluid between the conducting and glass layers. Without an electrical current, the rods fall into random organization and absorb light, whereas when a current is applied, they align to allow light to pass through. Unlike liquid crystal, suspended particle devices can be dimmed to allow for more or less heat and light. Both of these devices require a constant electrical current to maintain transparency whereas the third electrochromic system requires a current to effect a change in transparency, but the current is not required beyond that. These systems have generally been in use in small and medium-sized interior applications but are on the cusp of being available to the building industry for large-scale exterior application. The promise of a glazed tower wall with variable visual effects triggered by occupants who manage their own energy consumption and comfort is compelling.

Structural Glass

Beyond the failure of prismatic glass to prove sufficiently secure and blast-resistant for the Freedom Tower at Ground Zero, investigations of more widely applicable structural glass continue to move forward. These investigations are a part of the "lighter-faster-stronger" performative aesthetic which has, for some years now, driven architects to pursue larger spans of glass for window systems and to limit the metal framing systems required to support that glass.

Many of these developments can trace their roots back to early 20th century all-glass skyscraper visions like those earlier mentioned by Mies van der Rohe and Le Corbusier. With Norman Foster's 1975 Willis Faber & Dumas headquarters in the UK, the British glass manufacturer, Pilkington, initiated a set of technological innovations which began with glass patch supports and structural glass vertical fins, evolved to point-supported glass and spider clips, and has more recently delivered tension cable and rotule-support systems which eliminate primary column and beam structure as well as the sub-framing associated with glass support. These developments have generated a wave of enthusiasm for more glass and less supports which has persisted in the design community. Large expanses of glass window wall, dramatically cantilevered canopies, all-glass cubes, footbridges and floors have been the byproducts of research into structural glass. Its apotheosis today can be seen in the branded staircase of every Apple Store. "Ultimately, what we're all striving for is an all-glass structure,"[7] says James O'Callaghan of Eckersley O'Callaghan Structural Design, the engineers of the staircase.

Structural glass is almost exclusively manufactured from soda-lime glass, made, as it has always been, largely from sodium carbonate, limestone and silica. This is mostly the time-tested formula for conventional plate and cast glass familiar to us in everyday glass objects. Although there has long been a debate as to whether glass is a solid or liquid, considering its thermoplastic status, it is now usually described as an amorphous solid. The noncrystalline structure is achieved by rapid cooling below what is referred to as the "glass transition temperature," around 1,000 degrees Fahrenheit for the soda-lime variety. Cooled further and cut, plate glass is very strong but begins to lose strength the instant it's made. Tiny cracks begin to form through contact with other surfaces or even with water vapor and carbon dioxide.

"If you take the freshly made surface and blow on it with your breath, you've reduced the strength of glass by a factor of two,"[8] says Suresh Gulati, a retired glass specialist from Corning Glass. Even one gas molecule can break a silicon-oxygen bond in glass, generating a defect. While glass is strong in compression, tensile stresses will make these tiny fissures grow bond by bond, causing it to weaken or break. Protective coatings can work to protect against additional cracking although such coatings can affect

Willis Faber & Dumas Office, Ipswich, 1975 / Foster + Partners

Apple Store Fith Avenue, New York City, 2006 / Bohlin Cywinski Jackson

transparency. Alternatively, structural glass is frequently strengthened by tempering. This puts the surface under compression, so that even more tensile force is needed for cracks to grow.

For flat glass, heat tempering is most often used, on the principle that when glass cools slowly, it becomes denser. By cooling the exterior of a sheet and keeping the interior hot, the interior cools more slowly to a denser structure. This pulls the surface into compression, strengthening it. In chemical tempering, sodium ions in the surface are replaced with potassium ions, which are about 30 per cent larger and heavier. As the glass cools, it is constrained at its borders, so it becomes much more compressed, and stronger.

Although tempered glass may be much stronger and take longer to crack, it can still fail. Unlike other materials, glass does not deform in failure or otherwise give advance notice of imminent failure. Used as a structural element, this can have catastrophic outcomes. Thus, lamination is frequently used in various structural glass components. This usually consists of multiple sheets of tempered glass bonded with thin polymer interlayers to keep the glass together, acting in structural unity when properly functioning, and holding broken glass together when a sheet fails. Lamination makes fabrication difficult since cutting into tempered glass causes it to break. To avoid this, each sheet must be polished and drilled to receive its connections prior to tempering. Tolerances are very small to avoid potentially destructive stresses between the connections and the glass apertures.

Architects are investigating new shapes for their glass walls in an attempt to eliminate non-glass supports. Rob Nijsse, a professor at Delft University of Technology, and the structural engineering firm, ABT Belgium, has used large sheets of corrugated glass, mounted vertically for window walls in a concert hall in Porto, Portugal and a museum in Antwerp, Belgium. Other engineers are beginning to investigate clear adhesives to join glass directly to glass for structural applications. The increasing research in materials science and nanotechnology is promising, however, to date, long-term strength and reliability of adhesives have not been proven and building sponsors are wary of implementing them in tall buildings.

Additional Glass Treatments

<u>Coated Glass</u>. Coatings are often used to reduce solar heat gain to the interior of buildings. They are most efficient when applied to the second surface of the first pane of glass where they can immediately affect incoming heat and light and are less likely to be exposed to damage on the first, or exterior, surface. Occasionally they are reflective or darkened in order to address issues of glare (the relative brightness ratio of outside light to interior ambient light). While these coatings can be successful by day, in the evening when the relative brightnesses are reversed and the interior lights are viewed against a dark exterior, the coatings will generally result in high reflectivity into the interior space. This may be considered undesirable, particularly when night-time views are important: hotels and residential buildings are most fully occupied in the evenings. Glass coatings are also used in retail display installations where exterior glare can cause visual impairment. In these unique applications, they are typically applied to the first surface in order to intercept potential reflectivity to the exterior.

<u>Tinted glass</u>. Tinted glasses are glass sheets whose entire substrate has been tinted or colored. These glasses by necessity are manufactured to specific performance specifications as they have broad implications on the degree of light and heat which enters the building and, ultimately, the energy appetite of the building. The industry provides a narrow range of standard and often-used tints, however, an unlimited, and more costly, custom range is also available. Production costs decrease with large production runs so small custom orders can be difficult to realize. As a result, colored or tinted laminations have become popular whereby a double layer of glass sheets sandwiches a polymeric film (patterned, tinted or colored) within. Because patterns, tints and specific colors are now digitally created and manufactured, reliability and precision in a film is easy to achieve. These properties, however, have significant impacts on the transparency, reflectivity and solar properties of the glass.

<u>Frits</u>. High quality ceramic frit technology has been common over many decades as a way to opacify sections of glass curtain wall. The post-World War II drive to remake our cities a collection of glass boxes, yet accommodate the ever-necessary floor plenum carrying the vital engineering services they require, led to second-surface frits as a way

PG_67_PERFORMATIVE_SKINS.

Corrugated Glass

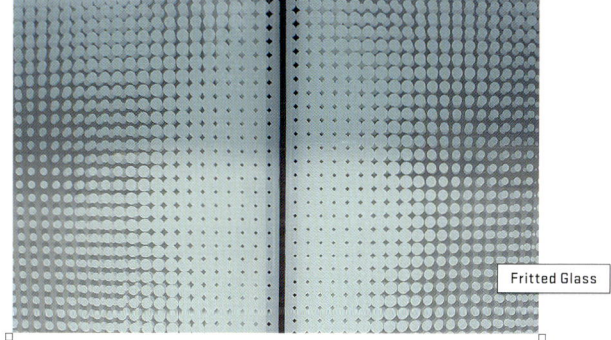

Fritted Glass

Films and Vinyl

Louvres, Melbourne Elm Apartments, Melbourne, 2010 / Elenberg Fraser

to opacify horizontal spandrels on every floor. By applying frit to the second surface of the same glass as the vision lite (tinted, coated or colored), both panes could be made to appear similarly, creating a monolithic look to the entire curtain wall. In the Post Modernism of the 1970s and 80s, further inventions explored recomposing glass facades with the broader use of fritted glass panels in both color and decorative patterns. In more recent times, our infatuation with architectural "layering," graphics, informational content and complexity has led architects to frit detailed and digitally rendered glass panels in an infinite array of custom applications. Some of the most recent experiments in state-of-the-art frits involve the efforts of research entities like the Lawrence Berkeley National Laboratory which is pioneering nanocrystal coatings capable of controlling heat, and possibly reflectivity, from the sun while maintaining glass transparency.

Films. The development of polymeric interlayer films for glass has been a natural outgrowth of films long used for glass in interior applications. With protection and the lack of exposure to weather, interior installations have included opaque and translucent films to achieve visual privacy and an array of decorative films which provided visual interest and, in some cases, relative degrees of privacy. Film products laminated to glass and other interior building materials have long been used for signage and various graphic systems. As energy costs increased, offices became computerized and green codes emerged, tinted and reflective films applied to the interior surface of exterior windows have become common ways to reduce solar

Louvres, Melbourne Elm Apartments, Melbourne, 2010 / Elenberg Fraser

Fabric (silicone)_ UBPA B3-2 Pavilion, Shanghai, 2010 / Studio Archea

heat gain and glare. The market for film products today has become highly specialized from light-diffusing films, to custom treatments and versions of everything that frits can do at a lower cost for a shorter life span. The omnipresent commercial advertisements which are regularly applied to building exteriors and METRO buses represent a portion of the expanding market for a durable material which can carry information while maintaining visibility from within.

Louvers. Louvers, as well as exterior wall systems with deeply-set fenestration, have long been an architectural feature of buildings that attempt to shield windows from solar heat gain and glare. While there are many configurations and versions depending upon the size of openings and the building's orientation with respect to the sun, horizontal louvers have generally proved effective for high sun through the middle of the day. For morning and afternoon hours where the sun is lower in the sky and rotating laterally in plan, vertical louvers have generally proved more effective. While these systems are designed in a range of building materials, many recent examples are designed in glass, sometimes treated with tints, coatings or screens and, occasionally operable to provide more responsive protection and to integrate with the building's natural ventilation systems.

Fabric Panels. While fabric panels are seldom used in the United States, many European examples exist. Commonly in arid and temperate climates, they are automated to close down when the sun is in direct contact with a window or opening. These panel systems share an affinity for the European tradition of multiple window coverings (interior

Metal Meshes, Caltrans District 7 Headquarters, Los Angeles, 2004 / Morphosis

Bent Glass, IAC Building, New York City, 2007 / Gehry Partners

drape, operable window sash and exterior shutter) and may become more viable long-term with advancements in synthetic and polymeric fabric research.

Metal Meshes. Metal meshes have been commonly used for many years. Generally limited to decorative and secondary applications, they have been applied to garage facades to shield cars and ceiling lights, elevator cab interiors for durability and for various tenant and retail installations to define specialty areas. Recently, these meshes have become more structurally stable, more variable in terms of materials, finishes and opening sizes, and now they are being fused with both photovoltaic cell and light emitting diode (LED) technologies which give them additional and valuable roles to play in a culture that places value on energy and information.

Bent Glass. Cold bending of glass is an emerging trend in glass facade design today. Contrary to the traditional method of heating glass within its thermo-plastic range prior to deformation, cold-formed glass is affected by forcing and securing the material in the bent shape during installation or by bending the glass in a frame and laminating it while in its bent form. The process produces glass free of the surface distortions resulting from heat forming but imposes additional stress on the material. The fluid and highly molded surfaces emerging out of design offices which use parametric modeling techniques suggest there will be continued interest in the ability to bend glass in tall buildings.

Building Integrated Photovoltaics (BIPV)

It has often been noted that the building sector makes up nearly 40 per cent of the world's demand for energy, and recent data indicates that buildings are, on average, poorly utilized. Tall office buildings are, in theory, occupied an average of eight hours a day five days per week. Absence due to business travel, holidays, vacations, illness and work breaks reduces this occupancy. When additional calculations are made, taking into account evenings and weekends, plus the effects of mobility enabled by wireless electronic media, the occupancy of individualized work stations and offices in these enormous buildings is between 10 to 20 per cent of a 24 hour seven day-a-week year. While these tall buildings require enormous quantities of energy to operate, occupied or not, they offer up huge glass surfaces from which to collect solar power. This being the case, skyscrapers are potential resources for net energy production from the sun. The technologies which enable this are referred to as building-integrated-photovoltaics or BIPV's and come in two particular classes.

The familiar crystalline variety is composed of silicon, a semiconducting material, which is typically fabricated in five-inch squares that are .012 inches thick. These squares are ganged together and laminated to glass in modules which can be applied to architectural surfaces. They are commonly the most efficient energy producers of the two crystalline types. The thin-film variety involves spraying a fine layer of semiconducting material to a sheet of glass, although stainless steel and plastics can also be used. Although this technique is the most wasteful of material and the most expensive to produce, thin film is a more fully integrated and custom product and is gaining popularity.

The majority of BIPV applications to date have been on tall buildings in Europe, Asia and the Middle East, where strong public support exists and substantial financial incentives are provided by their governments. Fewer inroads have been made in the US where the industry was pioneered in the 1970s with rooftop panels converting solar energy to heat domestic water. Two major reasons for the sluggishness of the American industry appear to exist. First, US code requirements state that BIPV hardware must be tested by a publicly registered laboratory. Historically, and as a practical matter, that has always been Underwriters Laboratories (UL). When any element in a solar assembly is altered, UL policy requires the retesting of the entire system. Abroad, however, when technologies are certified, minor changes do not require retesting and recertification. Another reason for the slower integration of these systems in the US is the lack of "feed-in tariffs," financial incentives to produce and feed energy back into the grid. This is perhaps the single greatest impediment to growth in the domestic industry. In many European locations, electricity can be sold back to the central power company at up to 4 times the cost; in other countries the sale price is higher. Conversely, in a US marketplace without financial incentives, many of the projects with the most vigorous solar energy systems are either public projects that are structured to afford these costs or theoretical projects that struggle to be built altogether.

There is a general consensus that in most countries, solar energy systems will reach grid parity within 5 to 10 years. At that point the economics for tall buildings which are held over the mid- to long-term, with or without incentives, should support widespread adoption of these systems, lowering the aggregate need for fossil fuel-based sources of energy.

Informational Facades

There has been a strong trend over recent decades in the direction of creating media facades on buildings of scale. By way of digital display technologies, the exterior skins of buildings, including tall buildings, have become surfaces projecting information of various kinds. These buildings with their extremely large surfaces, embedded with state-of-the-art LED systems display small pixillation and high resolution for still and moving imagery of exacting detail. There are many reasons for this trend, not the least of which is the increasing value of information in a commercialized Internet environment wherein the commercial tall building can be further monetized beyond its net rentable area. Although many aspire to a wider range of possible applications for this adaptive technology, the trend is largely being driven by the forces of commercial advertising. As a building skin is both an enclosure system and a public surface, this trend, in both concept and in practice, raises important questions about who controls the public realm and to what ends.

The concept of advertising, or media, architecture was first introduced into the critique of commercial buildings in the early twentieth century. Adolf Behne referred to Eric Mendelsohn's very successful department stores of the 1920s as "advertising architecture" for their use of broad bands of glass and light to display their contents at night and advertise the store's presence. Until that time, and thereafter, Modern architecture tended away from signage or additional visual communication beyond the elements of the building. As Robert Venturi noted in 1977, "Modern architects abandoned a tradition of iconology in which painting, sculpture, and graphics were combined with architecture...The message was mainly architectural."[9] Where signage existed in Modern commercial buildings, that signage became architectural, the informational content stylized as a visual object to be subsumed within the architectural character of the building.

An occasional rupture emerged in the taciturn surfaces of an evolving Modern architecture, allowing a building to express a wider range of content. "Media architecture" as a term has been used to reference Oscar Nitzchke's unbuilt Maison de la Publicite design for Paris in 1934. A steel frame was to be attached to the facade of a simple Modern rectangular building. On the frame, both fixed and neon images would be installed, available for rent to advertising agencies. Parodying the natural tendencies of the commercial building marketplace in locations such as New York's Times Square, Las Vegas and Tokyo, a later generation of architects from Venturi to Archigram asserted a vision of informational content dominating architectural space. These architectural visions were paralleled and informed by philosophers from the likes of Jacques Derrida, Jean Baudrillard and Guy Debord who deconstructed the relativity of language and understood the "sign value" of images and a society in search of spectacle. This realignment was one of several frontal attacks on the Modern Movement and one which, having had momentary impact in the 1960s and 70s, appears to maintain longer-term relevance in the critique of architecture and informational content going forward.

Paul Virilio has compared the current advent of media architecture to historic periods in which architecture and urban design were, in themselves, explicit communicators of social, and less commercial, values over the long-term. He has referred to the proliferation of media building screens and illuminated architecture as "Electronic Gothic," comparing them to Gothic cathedrals which conveyed static messages through the likes of stained glass windows, sculpture, tapestries and mosaics. The media surfaces of our tall buildings are now commercially available for rent and have the capacity and scale to transform our city squares, public plazas and boulevards into visually dense environments laden with fleeting commercial content.

Peter Cook's and Colin Fournier's 2003 Kunsthaus in Graz, Austria would have to be one of the first examples of the new media architecture. This large blue bubble of a building is made up of an acrylic outer skin oozing large "nozzles" which orient toward the northern sky to capture and admit natural light to the interior. The eastern facade is augmented with an additional feature called BIX,

Kunsthaus, Graz, 2003 / Peter Cook and Colin Fournier

Maison de la publicité, Paris, 1936 / Oscar Nitzchke

PG_75_PERFORMATIVE_SKINS.

Times Square, New York City

Las Vegas Strip, Las Vegas

a lighting concept developed by the Berlin-based architects, realities:united (realU). BIX is a matrix of a thousand flourescent lamps embedded in the eastern facade which can be individually adjusted for brightness over an infinite range of variability. As each lamp can be adjusted at the speed of 20 frames per second, images, films and animations can be displayed on the building's surface.

While the Kunsthaus carries a low-resolution imaging capability due to its limited number of lamps and their spacing, the Zero Energy Media Wall in Beijing, China prepared for the 2008 Olympics, contains a broader range of capabilities. On the face of the Xicui Entertainment Complex, this building at its completion represented the world's largest color LED display combined with the first fully-integrated photovoltaic system. The building was designed by New York architect, Simone Giostra in collaboration with ARUP and two German glass manufacturers. While the project as a prototype can theoretically carry any type of content, commercial or artistic, the Greenpix project, as it is called, initially included two curators who commissioned video works by artists from China and Russia.

The skin is a second building surface made up of glass panels laminated with polycrystalline solar cells and set at angles to maximize solar energy. These solar cells provide energy to approximately 2300 LED light points which are distributed throughout the wall for low resolution video art. The conceptual elegance of the system is that the solar cells collect energy during the day and feed the electrical needs of the lighting system by night. The brightness of the diodes depends on the weather and the degree of total solar energy available over the course of a given day. After an overcast day, the facade glows subtly at night whereas a sunny day results in a nocturnal display of intense color.

Sometimes referred to as Singapore's first urban entertainment complex, iluma is a mixed-use vertical project conceived as part of a 235 acre redevelopment master plan to transform an underutilized neighborhood into an arts, culture, educational and entertainment district. Completed in 2009, WOHA's Wong Mun Summ and Richard Hassell designed this project to incorporate multiple functions and to create a night-time magnet for a host of new neighborhood uses. iluma includes a parking structure, eight-screen cineplex and a top-floor theater for live performance in a 10 story structure. The building is alternately clad in solid and perforated aluminum panels as well as glass window wall. Like the architects for Graz' Kunsthaus, WOHA included in the team the contributions of Berlin's realU to incorporate media into the wavy glass facade of the architecture.

The applied skin, referred to as Crystal Mesh (CMesh), consists of 3200 polycarbonate and aluminum "crystals," tessellated and clipped to a steel support frame bolted to the building's exterior wall. Two thirds of the CMesh is illuminated by way of five foot and three foot wide hexagonal panels, each with up to seven individually dimmable compact fluorescent lamps inside. After dark, the polycarbonate crystals housing the fluorescent lamps become pixels in the programmable media facade controlled through an advanced European software system. CMesh requires custom-made content that accounts for the building's atypical wave-like design. Ultimately, the system could use sensor-based input to visually communicate observers responses through social networks, Website forums or mobile-phone technology. Designed as a dynamic prototype, the building's function and form aspire to interactivity.

Asymptote designed the Yas Hotel in Abu Dhabi with a molded canopy of steel and glass which similarly relies on LED luminaires to project video sequences onto fritted glass panels and their structural frame. The giant canopy shelters the two hotel slabs below from solar heat gain while providing visual content by night. Ben van Berkel and UNStudio have created similar effects on the Galleria Centercity in Cheonan, South Korea and at Star Place, Kaohsiung, Taiwan. Cultures that have long promoted buildings as carriers of illuminated content have embraced these LED-based skins which project vivid motion graphics. These installations forgo advertising and instead project spectacular light effects designed by video artists. Many of the casino communities from Macao to Las Vegas and Atlantic City to highly trafficked commercial zones in Piccadilly Circus and Times Square are rapidly adapting these technologies to supplant the skins of banal window walls with animated and illuminated messaging.

Iluma, Singapore, 2009 / WOHA

One of the most visible media walls recently installed is on the upper decks of the Port Authority Bus Terminal on New York City's 8th Avenue and 42nd Street. A2aMEDIA has designed, installed and operates the LED media display which went into effect in June of 2011 and has been expanded since. The interesting aspect of this Mediamesh system, produced in concert with GKD-USA, a German-based manufacturer of woven metal fabrics, is that it covers 6,000 square feet of building surface and renders high resolution motion graphics through embedded LED sources. The project features 16 panels containing 1.325 million LED diodes. The panels are made up of tensioned stainless steel metal fabric installed on two sides of the building. The density of the LED sources is such that they yield over 265,000 pixels, arranged approximately 2 inches apart vertically and 1.5 inches horizontally. This high resolution ensures complete daylight visibility and the spacing in the stainless steel mesh allows for the free movement of air within the parking structure, avoiding the need for mechanical equipment to control automobile emissions. Mediamesh design features 57 per cent open area, reducing solar heat gain as it provides for natural ventilation.

Star Place, Kaohsiung, 2008 / UNStudio

The Port Authority Bus Terminal, New York City

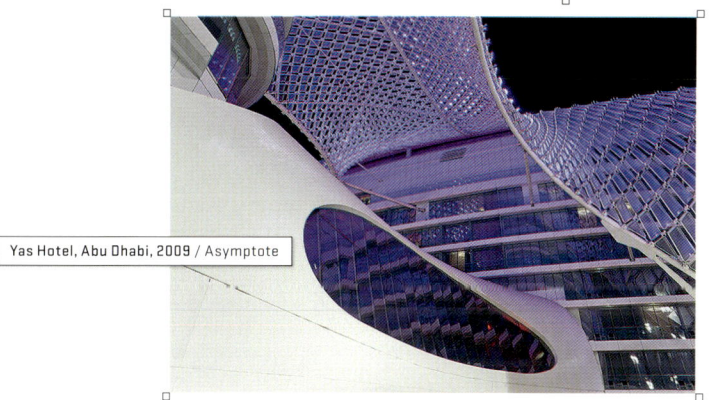

Yas Hotel, Abu Dhabi, 2009 / Asymptote

Galleria Center City, Cheonan, 2011 / UNStudio

[6] Schiler, Marc, *Performative Facades: A Proposed Definition*. Facade Tectonics: The Building Envelope 13, op. cit., 13.
[7] Fountain, Henry, *As Unbreakable as ...Glass?* The New York Times 7 July, 2009: op. cit., D1
[8] Ibid.,
[9] Venturi, Robert, Denise Scott Brown, Steven Izenour, *Learning from Las Vegas,* op. cit

CHAPTER THREE
PERFORMATIVE PARAMETRICS

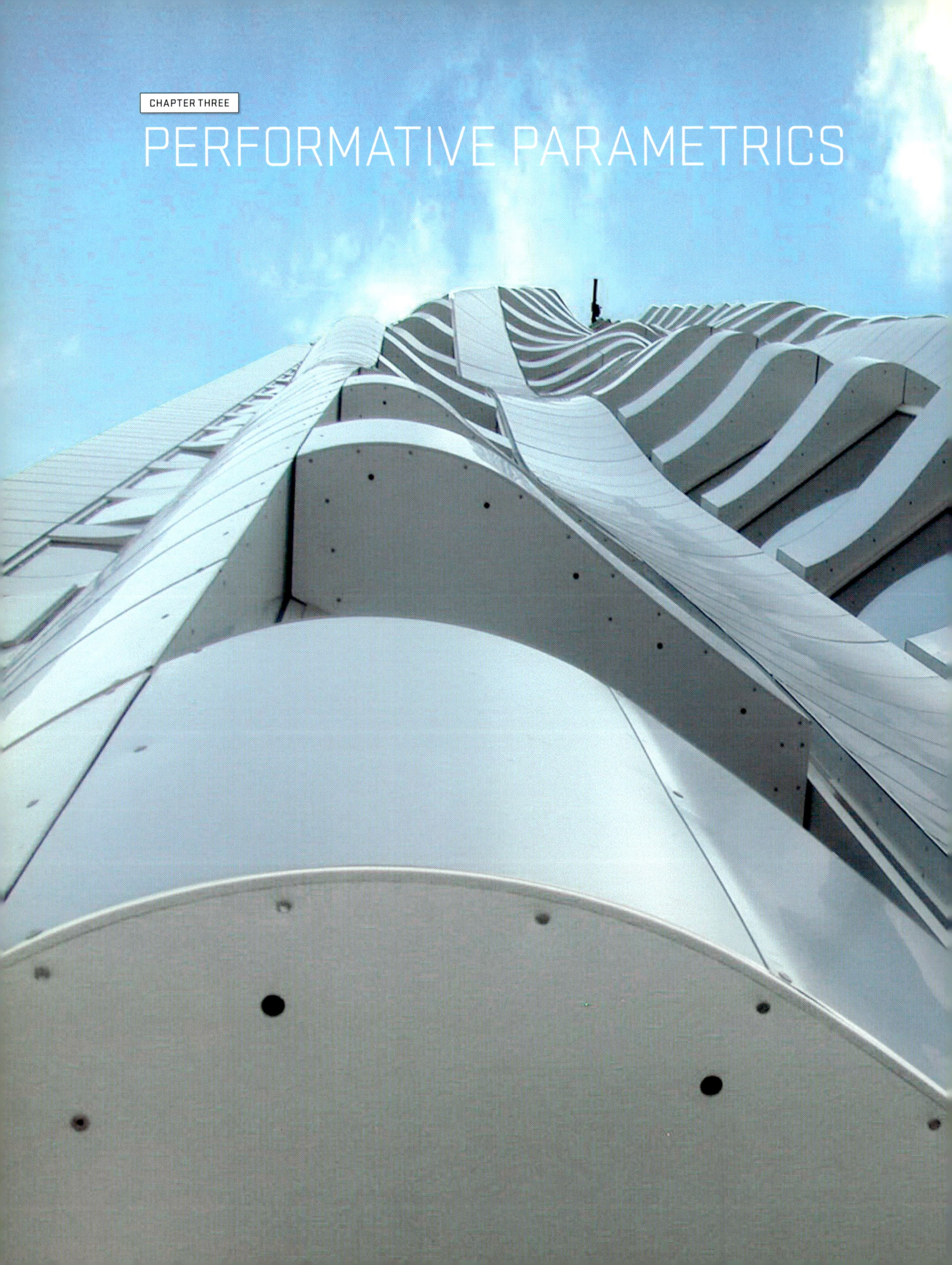

The current application of the computer to the creation of architecture has led to a wide range of names used to describe the phenomenon. Topological architecture, non-linear architecture, generative architecture, computational architecture and virtual architecture are familiar among the many. Because the process involves the digital programming of parameters and the measuring, revising, prototyping, and sharing of them, we will refer to the phenomenon as parametric architecture. In reality, architects have always been working parametrically, even without computers, which is to say that typically they have been given a program with parameters from which they have created a "model" that attempts to address those parameters. Because the design process has always been an inherently iterative act that simultaneously addresses multiple variables, design has always been a parametric process of shifting creative attention from initial scenarios that maximize individual solutions to final scenarios which attempt to resolve and optimize a fuller range of solutions. Now that computers provide complex digital modeling, a certain precision, speed and transparency has been added to the process.

Inasmuch as the tools and protocols inherent in parametric practices form a systems approach in which all variables are programmable, there is often a sense in the profession that higher levels of performance equate to more compelling, or more perfectable, architecture. The term, performance, is, in fact, highly qualified and refers strictly to the satisfaction of specific parametric goals. Human intelligence remains at the center of the design process, interpreting the data, directing the integration of goals and recalibrating them into conceptual solutions. Thanks to computers, parameters can be accurately programmed, tracked and measured but the determinants of exceptional architecture remain elusive.

Parametric modeling has overtaken the design of buildings of all scale and variety, however, the trend is nowhere more apparent than in new large-scale and tall buildings widely visible in the public realm. Because the tall building is known to be a building type which is resource-intensive with a potentially high degree of material and system repetition, great emphasis is naturally placed on parametric processes to both rapidly iterate design solutions and to insure precision, comprehensive coordination and high systems performance.

In *THE PARAMETRIC AFFECT*[10], David Gerber goes to great length to outline what is termed the "upstream" and "downstream" uses to which parametric modeling is put. Formerly a major tool of sophisticated industries such as airplane and automobile manufacturing, by the 1980s, the adaptation of Computer Aided Design (CAD) to architecture served as a representational device, enabling the architect to produce rudimentary drawings on a computer and to assist in three dimensional visualization. Since then, computer-based parametric modeling has developed to assist the architect in evaluating information-rich design concepts with speed, making it an ideal "upstream" tool for design investigation. It is, in this sense, a core tool in evaluating various design alternatives with respect to any parameters which have been programmed into the model. The act of design is transformed into a kind of highly-calibrated design iteration.

Through parametric modeling, the formal development of architecture can now be conceptualized, and materialized, through the lens of various performance goals such as daylighting, ventilation, acoustics, energy optimization and structural efficiencies. Once a design has emerged, parametric modeling can continue to operate as a "downstream" tool for the rationalization of the design whether that involves the integration of specialized architecture and engineering systems or the translation of non-linear shapes into constructible data. In fact, Gerber refers to these two parts of the overall parametric architectural process as "pre-rationalization" and "post-rationalization." Both applications are commonly used now in the design and construction of tall buildings.

In philosophic circles, the rise of the computer and its dominance in the creation of parametric form has caused a departure from twentieth century modernism's central dialectic of form versus function. A prevailing parametric belief holds that function, which is now more fully understood, measured and optimized, in fact, becomes form, which can now be thought of as one and the same, conjoined through a more continuous design process. Whether this is altogether true or not, the idea seems to create a number of challenges we can think of.

Patrik Schumacher, a director in the office of Zaha Hadid and outspoken proponent of a worldwide Parametric Style, argues for the "autopoiesis" of architecture which, he believes, is now fully enabled by parametric thinking. Autopoiesis according to Schumacher is "the self-referentially closed system of communications that constitutes architecture as a discourse."[11] He goes on to say that "there can be no external determination imposed upon architecture, neither by political bodies nor by paying clients, except in the negative, trivial sense of disruption." In effect, he asserts the notion that the power of architecture lies in its autonomy, its ability to speak to itself about itself. What he argues for, and believes that the design community is now ready for, is a "unified theory" of architecture based upon the broad and transformative impact of parametric systems.

Among the challenges this flight from pluralism poses is the division of architectural intent into two camps, one aligned with, what we will call crudely, the artistic impulse and the other, the social impulse. If, in fact, the dialectic of form versus function no longer exists, then this other dialectic of autonomy versus community may continue to be fought over for some time to come. It is not difficult to recall the manifestos of early twentieth century modernism which proclaimed a new architectural language that promised to address the social needs of an emerging industrial age. While many architects framed their work in the context of social progress, history has made clear that a new formal language was being developed, one which was frequently autonomous of contextual, let alone social, considerations. As is common to the fine arts, the aesthetic content of much of this work was primary: a sole architect operated as the principal visionary of the work much as an artist of the day did, and the work itself, although architecture, existed in a kind of autonomy both intellectually and spatially. This self-referential strain, now present in the Parametric Style as described by Schumacher, may prove to be an updated version of an ongoing debate.

Another challenge this proposal for an all-encompassing Parametric Style, or "unified theory", poses is to the prospect for differentiating architecture in a diverse and pluralistic world. The question of globalism is a concern in all fields: how homogenous is human experience in an age when communications, trade, travel and the appetite to consume appear universal? In architecture, does a global future portend a globally relevant "unified theory" in architecture or can we imagine the survival of meaningful cultural differentiation? In a uniformly Eurocentric moment of reflection, Schumacher counts Alberti's TEN BOOKS ON ARCHITECTURE, Durand's lectures on neoclassic architecture and Le Corbusier's TOWARDS A NEW ARCHITECTURE as history's preceding examples of unified theory. While he goes on to recall the sequence of European architecture's grand movements from modernism to post-modernism, deconstructivism and pluralism, he does not consider each of these meaningful and comprehensive aesthetic systems. In fact, he considers this diversity, a sense that the monolith of modernism has been replaced by a world of flux and fragmentation, "a historical illusion."

In recognition of his own post-structuralist evolution, Schumacher confesses to replacing his initial reliance on Marx's historical materialism as the dominant narrative with one based on the writings of Niklas Luhmann on systems of communication. Luhmann's work holds that contemporary societies are organized in terms of functional differentiation, that functional systems like politics, law, economics, science and art are parallel systems that co-evolve yet remain autonomous discourses. Science cannot instruct politics, politics cannot speak to art and economics exists in its own communication system independent of politics, for example. This functional independence which provides the foundation of Schumacher's notion of architectural autonomy, autopoiesis, may be attractive within the strict confines of a specialized field but unconvincing in a world where ideas are emerging from multiple sources and shared more broadly than ever.

Architecture and Metaphor

Architecture has always operated as a figment of likenesses. Whatever architecture is as an immediate and physical fact, it frequently aspires to meaning though its likeness to something else. This is the essence of metaphor, or metaphoric architecture. With the emergence of computer-based architecture and parametric thinking, at least two grand metaphors appear to have emerged.

The philosophy of Gilles Deleuze[12] and his version of what may be loosely called literary deconstructivism have been frequent reference points for theories about computer-generated form. Whereas the works of Michael Foucault and Jacques Derrida, two contemporaries of Deleuze, influenced architectural theory in their own times, it was later, with the rise of computers and virtual structures that the work of Deleuze became central to the discussion of parametric architectural theory. While literary deconstruction was generally used to disinter critical relations and intents in a written text, architectural deconstruction was oriented toward producing buildings which might subvert traditional formal compositions. With the advent of the computer, this subversion was both natural and complete.

In his writings, Deleuze introduced an agent he referred to as the Nomad. Obscurely described, the Nomad represents the independent and creative force engaged in an ever-unfinished philosophical and artistic project. The Nomad operates in opposition to the State, which plays a more passive role of capturing nomadic innovations, consolidating and adapting them to its own needs. The actions of the State induce the renewed aggression of the Nomad whose inventions are again absorbed in a never-ending cycle of co-dependence. Physically, Deleuze interpreted the Nomadic space as "smooth and heterogeneous" while he saw the State space as "striated and homogeneous." He illustrated smooth and heterogeneous space by likening it to the woven felt fabrics of the Mongolian nomads, smooth to the touch but consisting of dense entangled fibers. Further, Nomadic landscapes, he asserted, were smooth and non-territorial, merging one to the next as the travelers constantly relocated. Conversely, the landscapes of the stationary population of the State were striated with walls, enclosures and roads. In the age of the computer, these distinctions have been grafted to the field of contemporary mathematics wherein differential geometry describes non-Euclidean conceptions of space conceived without a discrete set of coordinates and capable of producing smooth folds defining curved space. This Nomadic field exists in natural contrast to the orthogonal matrix of containment, territory and striation, familiar to the State.

This brilliant dialectic conceived by Deleuze has conveniently provided architects of digital form a likeness by which they can describe their own works. Auspiciously, not only has Deleuze described a kind of visual outcome for his theories but he has also drawn a parallel between the historic life of the nomad and the borderless world of the web, open-source codes and file-sharing at the heart of today's parametric universe.

A second grand metaphor for parametric architecture has been the field of biomimesis. The complex interaction between biological form, material and structure has become a metaphoric way to think about architectural form in a parametric environment. Since 1917 when D'Arcy Thompson[13] wrote about the shapes of growing cells in terms of the mathematical and physical properties of living matter, there has been a recurring architectural interest in how living tissue self-organizes in order to respond to the forces acting upon it. During the 20th century, Antonio Gaudi, Frederick Kiesler, and Frei Otto were among the prominent architects who studied the likenesses of biological form and designed buildings and structures influenced by them. Their work represented a kind of biomimicry, the imitation of integrated biological form in the built environment. With the continued accumulation of scientific knowledge, a focus on the planet's limited natural resources and the capabilities of parametric modeling, architecture's likeness to biological form has firmly taken hold. As Ilaria Mazzoleni asks in *ARCHITECTURE FOLLOWS NATURE*, "How can architects and designers move beyond the formal imitation of nature to more sophisticated, nature-inspired, performance-based building design?"[14] Performativity is once again the goal.

Over time, biological organisms have evolved diverse patterns in which form, structure and material act upon each other. Their behaviors are so inter-dependent that they cannot be analyzed separately. Cellular material, which evolves to respond to a range of forces, is frequently organized at the microscopic level into seemingly randomized three dimensional polyhedra or as honeycombs organized in more regular parallel rows. Digital architects and engineers study these naturally-occurring patterns and attempt to analogize architecture in order to fully integrate building systems as biological matter does. While these investigations can focus on a complete integration of architectural function, their formal effects are often displayed in complex massing. Multi-dimensional and smart building skins which parametrically integrate environmental sensitivity with visibility and structure are also frequently the outcome.

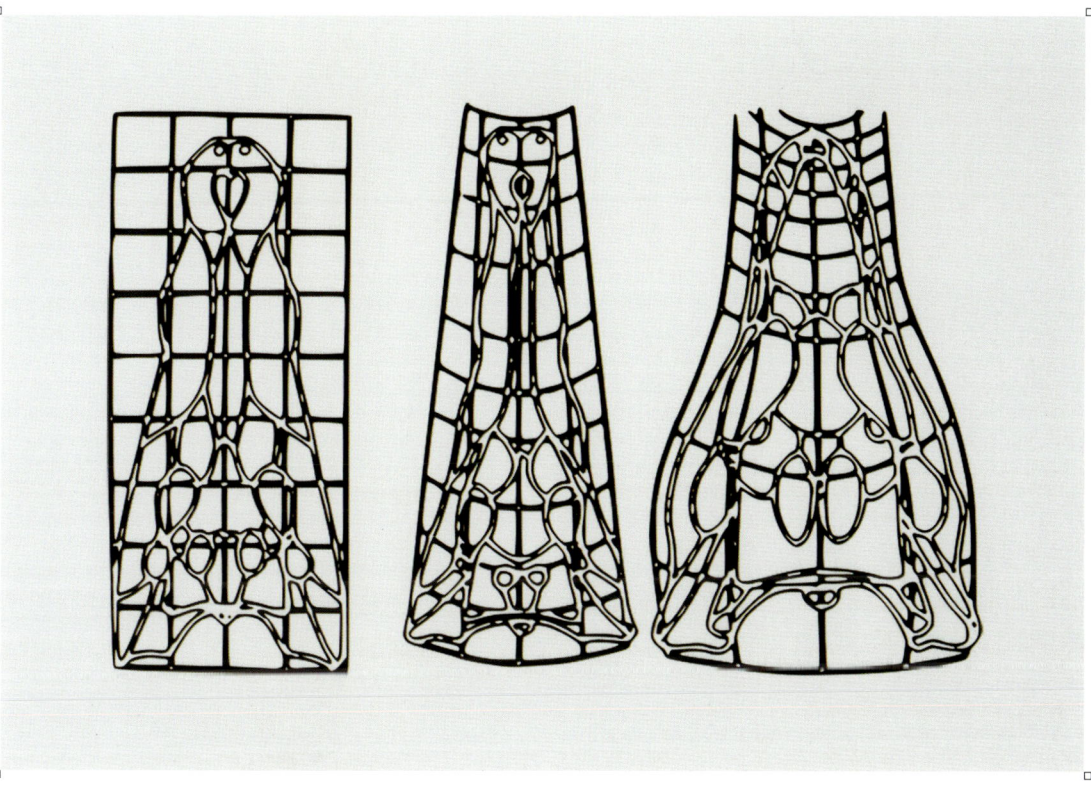

D'Arcy Wentworth Thompson, 1917

Practice

Most CAD software used by architects since the 1990s has been representational, meaning it has been a form of visualization. This, no doubt, is a translation of received protocols from earlier forms of drawing, physical modeling and visual communication. A new generation of parametric modeling software, however, is now transforming CAD from a visualization tool into a flexible and powerful approach to analyzing variables in a dynamic environment. This means that, in addition to being a visualization tool, modeling can be both a simulation tool and, at its core, an exploratory tool.

In addition to providing architects the ability to rapidly explore different design options, when combined with flexible Computer Numerical Control (CNC) fabrication techniques and digital analysis techniques such as Computer Aided Engineering (CAE) tools, parametric modeling expands the design possibilities for architects and reduces the time and costs involved in designing and creating custom building components and assemblies. Beyond that, modeling allows buildings to be rationalized with respect to performance goals such as daylighting, structural efficiencies, energy consumption, ventilation and acoustics.

Lisa Iwamoto has focused her efforts on the growing field of digital fabrication, extending our understanding that technology is "narrowing the gap between representation and building, affording a hypothetically seamless connection between design and making."[15] The computer has allowed architects to translate physical data from two dimensional drawings and three dimensional models into digital data that can communicate with a CNC machine. Now architects can model, represent, measure, revise, prototype, refine and fabricate in one continuous digital process.

Optimization is a key attribute of parametric modeling and the essence of performativity in design and construction. In parametric CAD software, an object's form and behavior are defined and constrained by a combination of its internal logic and its input variables. By embedding design, structure, fabrication and construction data in a parametric model, the entire design team can visualize form-making in architecture not as an a priori concept but as a complex and interrelated system involving many movable parts. Through optimization, a building designer can understand the organic relationship between performance information and formal outcomes, empowering him or her to determine the balance between performance goals, physical properties and formal gestures.

One of the most compelling implications of parametric modeling in general, and Building Information Modeling (BIM) in particular, is the impact it is having on the functional integration of design and construction teams. Currently, and in the standard design-bid-build construction contract, "means and methods" of construction are assumed to be the building contractor's responsibility. The architect's product, his or her design documents, are generally described as "for design intent only" and the architect's review of the building progress at the construction site is described as "construction observation." This distance between the architect's work and the actual construction process may be thought to provide a measure of legal protection for design professionals, however, it equally limits them from making meaningful decisions during the realization of the design. It also supports the fallacy that when design documents leave the hands of the architects, the design is complete and there are few if any requirements for ongoing creative communication, further design development or adaptation. This results in a construction environment wherein contractor selection is based upon lowest price, quickest schedule and maximum construction efficiencies. Most unfortunate is the inherently limiting and territorial positions designers and contractors inevitably take in a process in which the considerable knowledge base of builders, manufacturers and installers is divorced from the conceptual design process.

In the most conventional settings where parametric modeling is used today, architects are beginning to provide electronic files in the form of a Building Information Model (BIM) to contractors and subcontractors prior to construction for a more complete sharing of information. In more collaborative versions of design delivery such as Negotiated Bid, Integrated Project Delivery (IPD), Design-Assist, Design/Build and Multi-Party Joint Ventures, each member of the contractor/subcontractor team and the architect/engineering team can, in certain instances, be more fully integrated at the outset and share files. In this way, each informs the other with its own input and coordinates its work with other disciplines as the documents evolve toward higher levels of refinement and completeness. In addition to design and engineering coordination, these documents can also track additional parameters such as quantities, constructibility, budgeting and schedules

With parametric modeling, an important pedagogic change is underway whereby architects and students of architecture are learning to see design, analysis and fabrication as interdependent rather than separate and abstract processes. This kind of approach recalls the era of craft. For a craftsperson working intimately with materials and methods, feedback loops are created whereby aspects of early work affect later work, design is informed by its own construction, and technique and performance are cumulative. This is the kind of optimization which parametric modeling in its most complete version can provide.

A number of well-known firms have pioneered this trend toward collaborative modeling whereby the relationships between designers and manufacturers are jointly iterative. Gehry Partners supported by Gehry Technology made early strides in important building projects as have firms such as UNStudio, Foreign Office Architects and SHoP Architects. Historically, small-scale designers operating beneath the institutional radar have been favorable to craft due to their ability to oversee and control all aspects of design and implementation on small projects. While larger firms are pioneering many of the new platforms and protocols, if a smaller firm can afford the license or access the applicable programs, these new processes are ultimately available to all.

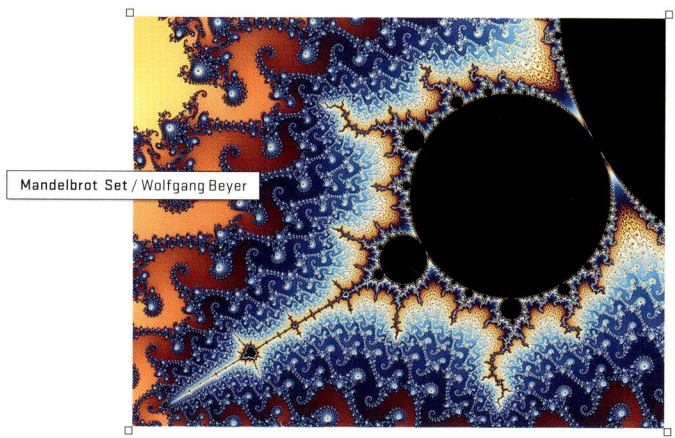

Mandelbrot Set / Wolfgang Beyer

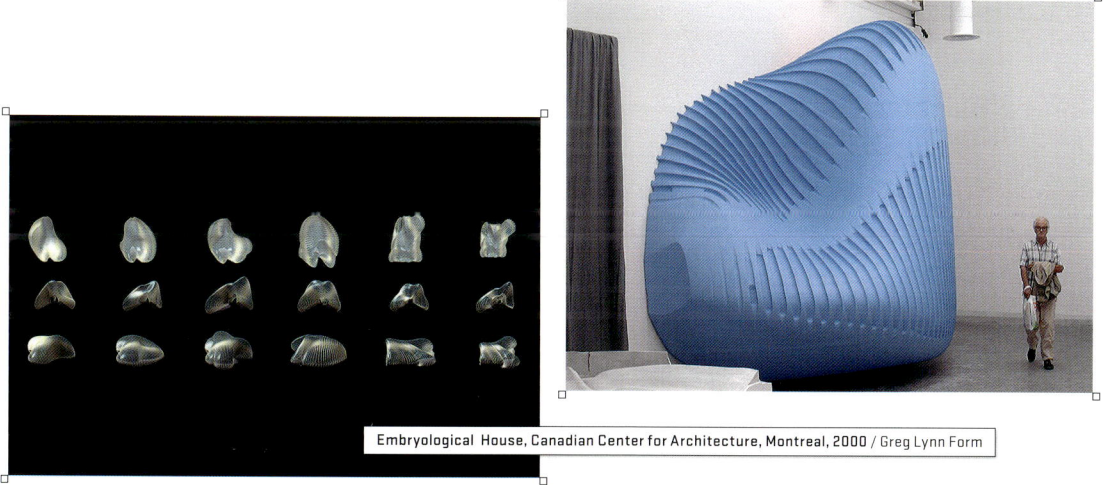

Embryological House, Canadian Center for Architecture, Montreal, 2000 / Greg Lynn Form

As Gerber and others have made clear, the computer did not invent parametric design, nor did it redefine architecture or the profession. It has provided a valuable tool that enables architects to design and construct innovative buildings with more exacting qualitative and quantitative conditions. The multi-warped surfaces of Gaudi, Mendelsohn, Otto and Kiesler were conceived prior to the adaptation of the computer but resonate both the optimization and formal outcomes of current parametric work. Architects had long observed nature and understood that plant life evolved to optimize its structural and metabolic requirements.

D'Arcy Thompson's work was followed by Alan Turing's 1952 mathematical models based upon biological patterns, keeping morphology alive as inspiration for architectural form. With Benoit Mandelbrot's 1982 studies in THE FRACTAL GEOMETRY OF NATURE[16], the computer emerged as a principal tool for simulating biological form and providing architects with a way to embrace parametric thinking. Conceived alongside early software developed for the aerospace and automobile industries, architectural parametric modeling came into its own in the 1990s.

Many architects have advanced our understanding of the possibilities of parametric modeling. Greg Lynn and Tom Wiscombe have pursued form-making based upon genetic systems and codes while the Architectural Association's Design Research Laboratory (AADRL) and Emergent Technologies and Design (EmTech) programs stood at the center of international experimentation and research on the subject as early as the 1990s. The earlier interest in fractal geometry evolved toward tessellated patterning which soon

Huaxi Urban Centre Tower, Guiyang, 2008 / Tom Wiscombe Design

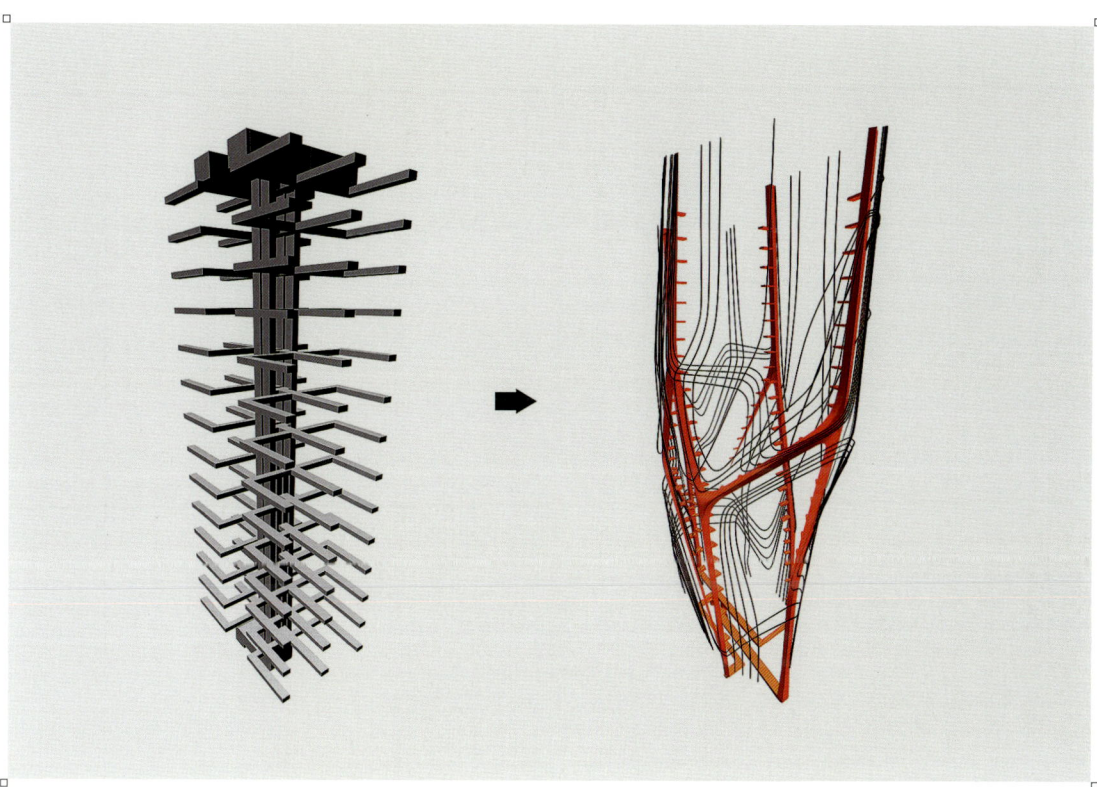

became a common method to structure complex organic forms in architecture. Complementary aesthetic theories on ornament, decoration and beauty subsequently found a place within current architectural discourse. At the level of practice, developments in computer programming and scripting have facilitated structural tiling and patterning sequences which characterize much of the present-day interest in animating complex architectural surfaces.

Defying Categories

When I began to conceptualize this essay on parametric applications to tall buildings, I entertained the notion of organizing the discussion of modeling in categories. The thought was to categorize software systems according to their affinities for characteristically generating specific formal outcomes. In thinking about tools, one considers the relationship between early modern architecture in the beginning of the 20th century and its relationship to industrial tools and products. Architects themselves drew a likeness between the productively organized and sanitary conditions of the industrial environment and its parts and the image of architecture. Focusing on clean lines, white, sun-washed surfaces, and the explicit representation of programs and circulation, it was no surprise that Le Corbusier, a lover of autos, machines and factories, referred to the house as "a machine for living."

Following World War II, technological developments again inspired a likeness between technical means and methods and architecture. Large-scale mass production, a staple of the war effort, encouraged an interest in architectural pre-fabrication and modularity. The development of new materials such as aluminum, engineered for lightweight aircraft, transferred to building panelization and curtain wall systems. Larger panes of stronger glass, high-strength steel and plastics all fed the vision of modern architecture and its furnished environment.

And so it seemed reasonable at the outset to look at the emergence of the computer and assume that various software tools could be grouped with others in terms of inevitable, or at least, easily-derived formal outcomes in architecture. Working through this premise with a number of the more advanced modelers in our studio, however, proved problematic. While we could identify the beginnings of each major software application and characterize it with respect to its initial attraction and success, it was less clear now, some years later, that software programs are today generally distinct in terms of outcome. It is easy, for example, to identify the unique and early transfer of Maya, Rhino and 3D Studio Max from the world of animation and gaming to students and architects interested in the fluid forms, topographies and "soft body" qualities of the programs. It is easy, in retrospect, to recall Frank Gehry's early adoption of CATIA from the aerospace industry as a method to digitize and translate form from physical models to digital models, then building documents and, ultimately, built form. And one can see the unique purpose behind AutoDesk's creation of REVIT as a method to rationalize material qualities and quantities and share information among a number of design and construction team professionals.

In their historic inceptions, these software systems were unique and their outcomes were specific and identifiable. When, however, our team of modelers considered the present-day output of graph-based systems such as Grasshopper or Generative Components, stack-based systems such as 3D Studio Max, associative history-based systems such as Maya or the various BIM softwares, distinction was less clear. Surveying the output of various architects and design firms who employ different systems, it was not often obvious which systems created which outcomes. In fact, a second point, perhaps as important as the first, is that the outcomes tended toward uniformity and it appeared to us that programs are developing "toward the middle." Conformity in parametric form generation may represent some informal consensus between digital capabilities and aesthetic preferences in our age, some kind of technology-fueled Zeitgeist, a phenomenon not unfamiliar in other periods of architectural history. In addition to that, a software development trend "toward the middle" may mean that the dominant commercial marketplace for these systems is causing programs generally used for conceptual design iteration (pre-rationalization) to attempt to capture additional market share in building documents and constructibility (post-rationalization) while the programs generally used for the latter purpose are attempting to widen their applicability to include the former.

Next we will examine the application and outcome of

Aeon II, Dubai, 2008 / Reiser + Umemoto, RUR Architecture P.C

Absolute Towers, Mississauga, 2012 / MAD Architects

parametric design in three projects, two as yet unbuilt and one built. Each is a tall building representing a distinctly different building type. Aside from common elements such as vertical circulation, structure and multi-functional skins, programmatic requirements for each is dramatically different. The first, a stacked vertical mixed-use tower by UNStudio sits atop a commercial retail center in Hangzhou, China. Each zone has specific and differentiated needs yet systems must be optimized vertically to resolve those differences. Phare Tower by Morphosis in Paris has been widely published and straddles a transit concourse with a hybrid structure at its base but is essentially a uniform and speculative office building from the ninth floor to the top. Gehry Partners' 8 Spruce Street, formerly known as Beekman Tower, in Lower Manhattan, while combining limited mixed-use programs at its base, is almost exclusively a residential apartment building, a program which is inherently cellular, attempting to resolve view orientations and a specific unit size distribution while maximizing net rentable area.

Raffles City, Mixed-Use Tower in Hangzhou

This 400,000 square meter project composed of two 60 story mixed-use towers represents CapitaLand's sixth Raffles City. The distinctively fluid shapes which include twisting and hybrid forms contribute a distinctive look to the otherwise conventional and burgeoning lakeside city of Hangzhou. Obviously impressed by the qualities of the natural landscape and its intersection with a growing urbanism, Ben van Berkel says that he wants to "give this concept

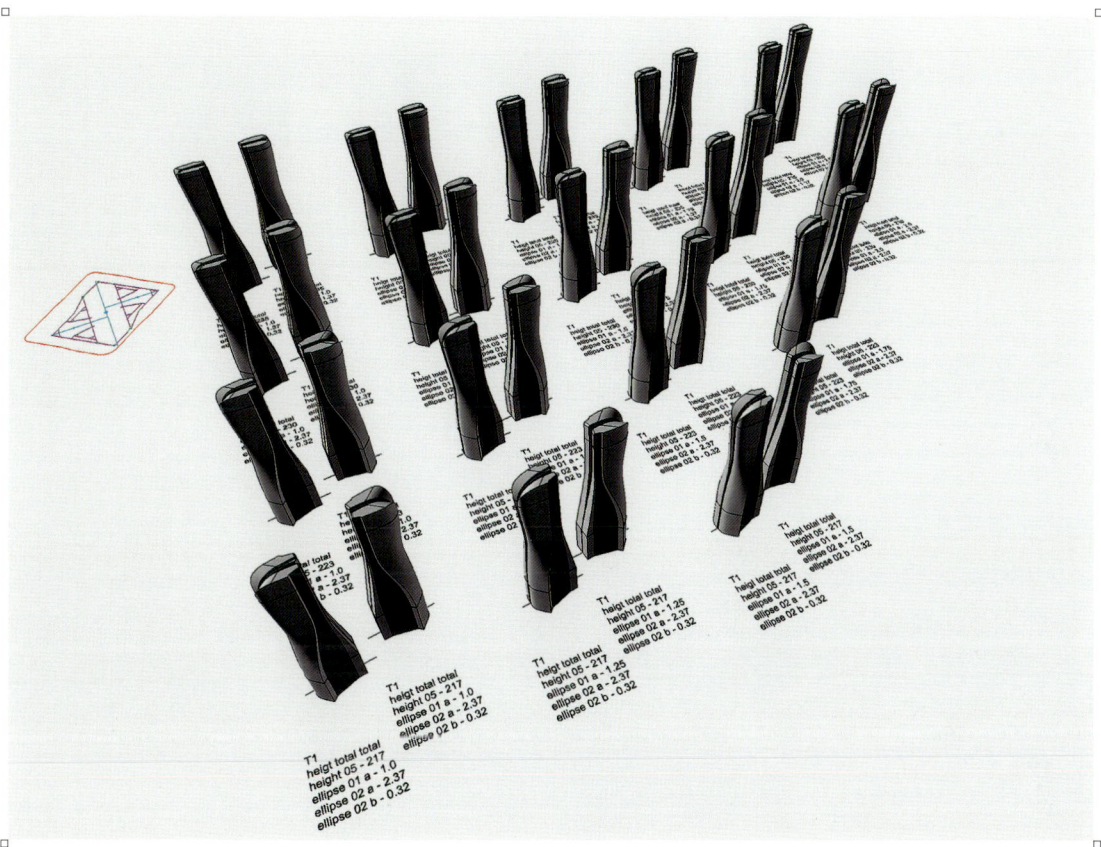

Raffles City, Hangzhou, Under Construction, Planned realisation of podium 2014 / UNStudio

a twist; by focusing on where the urban context meets the landscape of the city. In the design of the towers the urban element of the project twists towards the landscape, whilst the landscape aspect, in turn, twists towards the urban context, thereby effecting the incorporation and consolidation of these separate elements in one formal gesture."[17]

The program for the two-tower structure includes multiple below-grade parking levels and a super-block size seven story retail plinth above which sits two towers each of which contain residential/guest units atop office floors. Despite the fluid forms and hybrid shapes, the scheme is based upon a simple cruciform plan oriented diagonally in a rectangular block. The two towers are sited opposite each other to maximize light, air and tower views with the central axis of the retail mall bisecting them and running in the transverse direction. In this manner, the mall functions conventionally with a central vertical circulation element naturally lit from above, equidistant from the anchor ends of the mall and the lobbies of the two towers in the other direction. At the ends of the mall, natural light is admitted from above, as it is at the base of each tower which is sheared away to allow light to penetrate each tower lobby. At five major locations within the block-sized podium, a view of the sky and natural light penetrates the mass of the project.

Ground floor access into the bottom of the mall is at mid-block, reinforcing the orthogonal grid of the city, yet immediately re-directs the visitor into the diagonal grid of the mall and tower arrangement. Accordingly, the project reflects a somewhat superficial regard for the urban landscape of the city at its exterior and creates its own "city within a city" and its own autonomous urban design strategies and formal logics.

The massing of the two towers and their outwardly similar appearances belie the actual differences in the programming of their floors. Clearly there is an attempt to create twin iconography. One tower contains 16 floors of office with six floors of rooftop penthouse residences above twenty-four floors of hotel, while the other contains 12 floors of office with serviced and strata apartments above that. The overall effect of the towers is one of two twisting vertical shafts bilaterally symmetrical about the axis of the mall below. In fact, the creation of the twist is a carefully calibrated layer of the skin wrapped around an essentially rectangular floor plate which circumscribes the inevitable rectangular vertical circulation core.

Because the elevator core in the lower section of the tower must be sized to contain all the elevators (office, hotel, apartments), and the floor depths required for effective office plans are large, the bulge in the bottom of the towers is a fluid attempt to accommodate these metrics. As the floors then reconfigure and recede in size to suit a residential or hotel floor and to acknowledge the reduction in core requirements (the office elevators have dropped off below), the shafts of the towers reduce in length. Additionally, a superficial layer of the massing parametrically rotates around the long axis of the buildings, giving them the sense of twisting without fundamentally altering the plan diagrams. This twist is mirrored with a change in window wall design, further reinforcing the sense of rotation.

In an example of the algorithmic fusion of multiple design strategies possible through parametric modeling, the incremental twisting floor-by-floor of the two principal tower window wall systems represents both a formal predilection by the designers as well as a calculus with respect to optimizing natural light and solar heat gain. In the generally east and west directions where the sun is flat, a perforated metal shading system is maximized in the vertical direction. Adjacent to that system is the vertical window panel which provides light and view to the building interior but is shaded by the adjacent panel. As each tower wall rotates into the southerly direction, the vertical shading panel incrementally rotates diagonally until it becomes horizontal, the optimized orientation for shading high sun from the south in the middle of the day. This incremental migration is based upon algorithmic data and implies considerable customization in the building. Nevertheless, outcomes such as these are becoming more achievable as all facets of the design and building process are digitized.

The second principal window wall system is a floor-to-ceiling horizontal expanse of glass. This system is oriented to the south and includes broad terraces for outdoor activity and landscape along the height of each tower. Each terrace acts as a horizontal shading device for the inset glass wall below while preserving direct sun to plantings at the front edge of its terrace. Solar heat gain is reduced while indoor/outdoor activities and views are maximized. Further, in a nod to the greening of towers in Asia, to which Ken Yeang has dedicated a career, UNStudio's stated desire to bring sunlight and landscape from the ground level up the full height of the towers has a chance of being realized.

Raffles City, Hangzhou is one strong example of what is possible and what limitations exist within an evolving set of parametric practices. Notwithstanding declarations regarding contextual intentions, the project certainly radiates a high measure of formal autonomy at least at the most obvious levels, the plan parti and the formal image of the buildings. Also, as program requirements of a project of this size and commercial nature dictate, the overall massing and stacking is conventional: multi-story linear retail mall with three points of light and vertical access, towers split with access from mall and from street corners. Each tower shares vertical circulation per use with sky lobbies to minimize core size and segregate occupants.

There is a clear prerogative on the part of the architects to synthesize the inherently different characteristics of each vertical use into equivalent shapes. It would be arguable that the window conditions and their public/privacy implications might be different per occupancy, floor-to-floor heights would naturally vary, floor depths and the expression of full floor office tenants versus the more repetitive bay widths of hotel guest rooms or residences could be expected. Notwithstanding the many inherent differences, the overriding intention is to smooth these into two equal towers, uniform and integrated in shape, skin and image. With the advent of parametric modeling, the ability to achieve this in a shape of such complexity is both conceivable and

PG_95_PERFORMATIVE_PARAMETRICS.

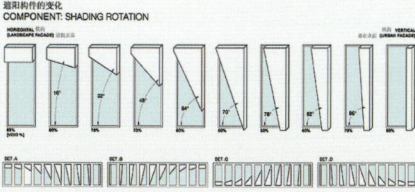

Raffles City, Hangzhou, Under Construction, Planned realisation of podium 2014 / UNStudio

realizable; however, the desire for such uniformity cannot be seen to grow out of the program nor the technology. With parametric tools, the architects can now create the software, model, measure and optimize an array of goals and then document the seemingly infinite calibrations the design requires. While the ability to create fluid form is certainly enabled by the technology, the desire to employ it formally in this way is an a priori mandate of the architects.

Phare Tower, Office Tower in Paris

Descriptions of Paris' proposed Phare Tower by Morphosis, the building's architects, states that the project's overriding goal is to synthesize the idiosyncrasies of its fragmented site. In a recall of the "space of flows"[18] of Manuel Castells' capitalist theories, the secondary goal, according to the architects, is to "express the multiple flows of movement" in the area. The site for the 66 story 300 meter office tower is in La Defense, a high-rise office center located two miles west of Paris. Since 1958, when they were banned from the central city, high-rise buildings have been located along the Peripherique and in districts such as La Defense, a zone of isolated contemporary towers frequently set within characterless open plazas. Notwithstanding the desire to create a mixed-use neighborhood, the preponderance of office buildings has made La Defense environmentally repetitive and vacant after hours.

The tower emerges from a highly irregular site bordered by an automobile motorway and a rail connection. An existing pedestrian concourse bisects the site and serves as a ground-level link between the 1989 Grand Arch of La Defense and the 1958 CNIT building, formerly an exhibition hall for the National Inter-University Consortium for Telecommunications. Circulation is planned to be routed from the existing below-grade transit station through the CNIT building and into the tower's public spaces by way of a new pavilion, a part of the Phare Tower construction. The structural design of the new building employs three primary structural legs, one landing near CNIT, opening up to Place Carpeaux and preserving a pedestrian view corridor to the Arch.

Although the building program is principally an office tower with the minor addition of cafes and retail amenities, the design of the project's base and ground plane attempts to integrate the circulation and public open space vectors acting upon it and lift these basically horizontal activities along a vertical axis up into the tower. Glazed escalators run from the plaza level pavilion along the third structural leg and up to the ninth floor where a Grand Hall receives all tower visitors and provides central security and access to elevator banks. Two mid-rise and rectangular massing elements (the East Building and the westerly Trapezium) abut the shaft of the main tower and contain two of the structural legs which support it. These lower elements mirror the more conventional office building neighbors in the area.

While complex factors have been identified and used as the basis for design in the lower register of the building, the middle and upper sections of the tower are smooth and simple, bulging slightly to contain the Grand Hall and then subtly tapering and rotating over its height to reflect the reduction in elevator cores, the consequent reduction in floor plate size and a range of other factors. The northerly wall, in contrast, abuts a major city street and is vertical and completely flat. At the top of the building a cluster of antennas and a crown of wind turbines adorn the skyline.

The effects of digital programming and parametric modeling are broad on this project and demonstrate both adaptive strategies as well as the limited impacts possible on this particular building type. The conceptual design process at Morphosis shows that, in response to the siting and massing intricacies described above, dozens of 3D models were produced in a rapid-prototyping effort, testing priorities and their formal outcomes to the many contextual conditions at the site. While this kind of prototyping can be used in any conceptual design process, its speed is particularly helpful in a competition timeframe where solutions at one level (massing for example) must be identified quickly so that more detailed development (refined massing, detailing, and skin development for example) can follow.

But given the limitations of massing inherent in a tall office building, some of the most compelling effects of parametric modeling in the Phare Tower are in the various and interrelated ways in which the detailed massing and surfaces were mapped and developed. To a designer of tall commercial office buildings, a wide range of performative goals present themselves throughout the design and refinement process. In addition to the rentable areas per floor, optimum lease

Phare Tower, Paris, Planned Completion 2017 / Morphosis

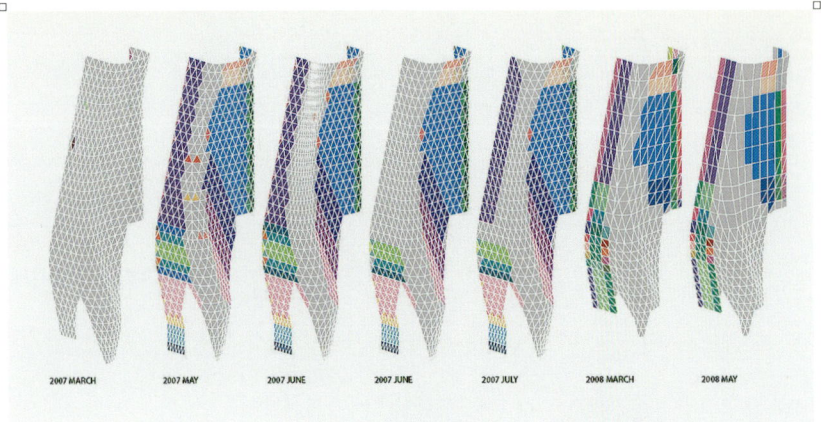

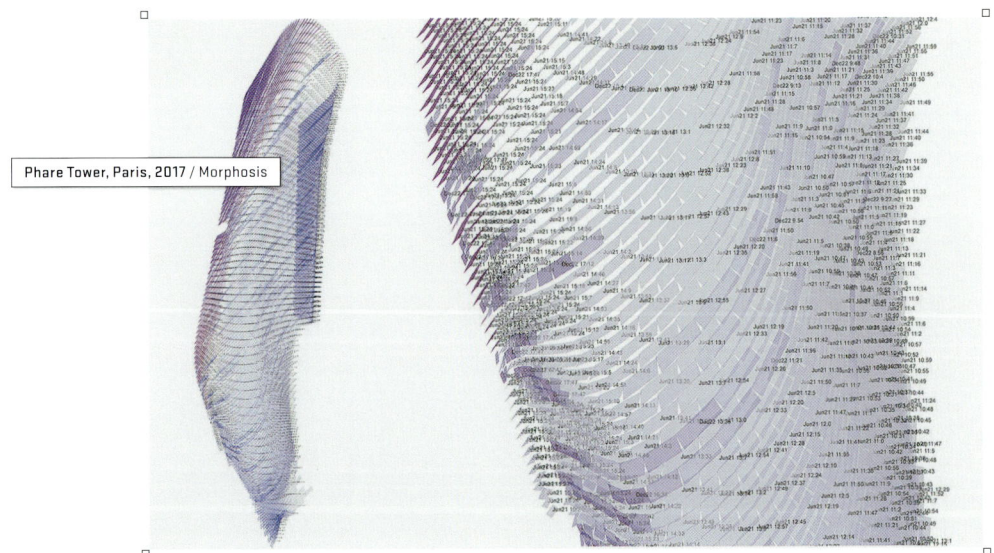

Phare Tower, Paris, 2017 / Morphosis

depths, floor efficiencies and configurations, space planning modules and applicable codes, the tall building is subject to the physical elements in ways that shorter buildings are not. Some of these are the wind forces which need to be mapped and modeled, solar heat loads, quantities of natural light to the building interior over the course of the day and year, possible shading and its efficacy, preferred views, their relationship to value and the efficiencies of structural design, something which is fundamental to the building architecture and can impact cost in a substantial way.

Working from the inside to the outside, Morphosis has conceptualized the structural system as a steel diagrid, a system that has been pioneered in tall buildings by firms such as Foster + Partners and occasionally, OMA. The diagrid provides efficiencies, particularly in the case of hybrid forms and when large volumes or surface areas create irregularities in the overall massing. In these cases, the diagrids, through triangulation, disseminate stresses more uniformly around these irregularities, like a structural skin or blanket. The conventional and less efficient frame of column and beam, which would be highly customized in the case of the Phare massing, is subsituted for a structural "skin" which can be plastically matched to the outer layer of building skin. Parametric modeling of structural efficiencies and loads have long been used by structural engineers and have been applied here to optimize structure with surface form.

Initial competition sketches for the tower showed a uniformly glazed skin which has undergone considerable design development since that time. Current digital drawings represent parametric modeling techniques which both map and optimize solar heat loads and rationalize the number and size of glazing panels which will need to be produced to cover the tower. This process of rationalization shows a design chronology in which triangular faceting (tesselation) was originally conceived, then categories of radially faceted glass and flat sections of glass were identified, and finally a highly optimized classification of optimized glazing panels based upon a precise relationship of form to surface was created. In a building form of this complexity and irregularity, only parametric tools could achieve the final outcome.

Finally, the latest renderings and computer drawings indicate that the outermost skin is a diagonally-oriented stainless steel mesh which is suspended off the face of the curtainwall and separated by a catwalk for access. Like the glass panels, these woven mesh panels have been analyzed and then optimized into families but all are flat and rectangular, approximating the curvature of the building enclosure through incremental variations in the panel joints. Thom Mayne's declarations that the tower will look alternatively transparent, translucent or opaque refer to the iridescence of the outer skin as viewed from different angles.

Kerenza Harris of Morphosis explains that the project was begun on Bentley software from Microstation. During the development of the design, the office hired a programmer to write script for a customized parametric model of the building. The design has been in development for several years now and subsequent to that, Morphosis gained access to Digital Projects (DP) which has become, according to Kerenza, formerly of Gehry Partners, such a powerful tool that one person can now do the work of two or three. The architects continue to use DP in the office on new projects.

Notwithstanding its level of invention, Phare Tower is still a commercial speculative office tower. The constraints of the building type are considerable and yet have been explored and redefined in dramatic ways. The massing is responsive to the program but is altered as it identifies new design cues. The base of the building is highly complex and whether it actually clarifies existing conditions or adds new layers of meanings to them, the formal outcomes are expressive and enabled through unconventional thinking applied through parametric tools at many levels. Finally, the multi-dimensional performance and appearance of the building's several skins takes the more rudimentary lessons of earlier Morphosis projects and advances them in this tall building.

8 Spruce Street, Residential Tower In New York City
Originally referred to as Beekman Tower, 8 Spruce Street, Frank Gehry's New York City tower is his first tall building proposal to be constructed. While the 76 story stainless steel building sits atop a seven story masonry base containing a school, offices and minor amenities, the tower portion itself is exclusively a residential apartment tower. At its opening, 8 Spruce was the tallest residential building in Manhattan. The project is, in many ways, a conventional program. A T-shaped plan, the tower sets back three times and is vertical and flat along its northern boundary. As the building sets back, the core migrates and the number of residential units reduce. While Gehry has been known for some of the most exuberantly massed buildings in his generation, the design of this tower, reminiscent of his 2007 proposal for a Mandarin Oriental Hotel at Los Angeles' Bunker Hill, has been focused on a simple massing concept and an elaborately sculpted wall system.

While this phenomenon may seem uncharacteristic of Gehry's many cultural and public projects, the programmatic realm of commercial housing is emphatically tied to residential unit sizes and amenities, a specified blend of unit types, efficiencies, price points and current market data. It is not uncommon for established residential developers to set forth all of this criteria including residential unit prototypes, key dimensions, furnishings and appliance standards while an architect of note and skill such as Frank Gehry works to identify those elements which can be introduced into the project, giving it unique qualities and signature status.

The key design element in this project is clearly the skin and the building's public success illustrates the relative importance of skin on a tall building which projects its identity on the skyline of the city. It is widely known that much of Gehry's work grows out of a historic effort to construct physical models. In the 1990's, the office adapted CATIA, a computer software program developed for the aerospace industry as a way of transferring physical

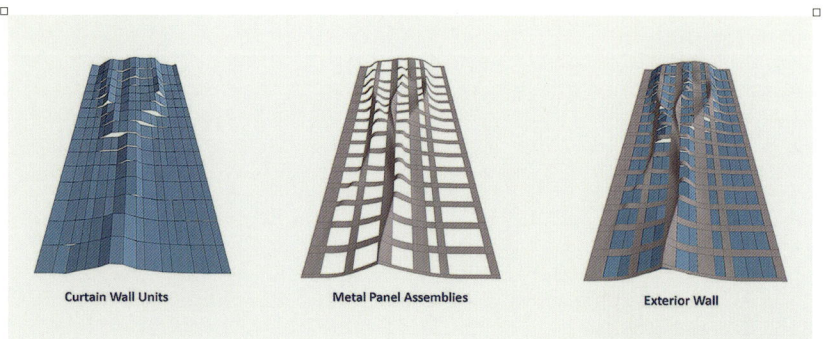

8 Spruce Street, New York City, 2010 / Gehry Partners

8 Spruce Street, New York City, 2010 / Gehry Partners

models into computer modeling and documentation. Early massing studies for 8 Spruce from the Gehry office suggest that at the outset, there was a wide range of modeling studies done which investigated the fundamental massing of the tower, much as Gehry might do on any project. Among the many models executed, an interest in tortile folds persisted. Many of the models recorded were either full-on or partial serpentine columns. Initial study models showed clusters of bundled towers with no setbacks, others faceted while still others showed curved forms. This process appeared to be the familiar Gehry process of building physical models for evaluation and testing them through parametric modeling for their prospective relationship to the requirements of the stacked residential floor plans. Eventually, the three steps appeared and the curved folds of the final building design were further studied. Gehry has likened the wall design to the "hard folds" of the Baroque sculptor, Bernini, and he has achieved them in the soft undulations which appear to float across the tall surfaces of the tower but resolve at sharp splines which are visible in the light effects of the stainless steel skin.

In addition to the close relationship between architectural design and residential planning, design delivery was executed in the form of "design assist" in which the construction manager (KBF), curtain wall fabricator (Permasteelisa North America) and other consultants shared software modeling data during design to tightly integrate the roles of all parties. Also, Gehry Partners (GP) added Gehry Technologies (GT) personnel to the project in the conceptual phase so that they could provide production continuity and construction interface following design. At the Gehry office, design schemes were modeled in the familiar way, from physical models, to Rhino datum surfaces, to CATIA. While the design engine was first built in the CATIA V5 platform, it was later moved to Digital Projects once DP was introduced into the office. Other consultants interfaced on CATIA, SolidWorks for parametric modeling and AutoCAD for submission to Gehry Partners for review and coordination.

Due to the application of such a complex skin to a conventional building type, three fundamental constructibility decisions were made which improved the prospects for coordination and performance. First, a unitized curtain wall system was selected over a stick-framed window wall because of the limited site area available to assemble wall sections. Additionally, wall assemblies could be factory manufactured and inspected and shipped ready-to-install to the project. Second, rather than a conventional exterior wall which would be waterproof, the decision was made to create a rain screen with a typical air-and-water barrier positioned behind the undulating wall. Stainless steel sheets were riveted to aluminum rain screen sub-frames and attached to flat unitized curtain wall panels which could be transported and erected with some ease. Finally, while the windows move in and out in concert with the folds of the exterior skin, the decision was made early on to keep all windows flat. Notwithstanding that decision, it was necessary to design a structural slab system that follows the undulations of the skin with the slab edge. Ensuring that the 14,000 embedded aluminum brackets at slab edge all matched to the receiving panels was another advantage of a shared computer platform between design and construction team members.

David Gerber, in his studies of the Gehry office, concludes that the vigorous amount of design exploration on 8 Spruce was specifically enabled by the parametric template used. He says, "it provides detailed analysis of the cause and effect of the formal design upon the data, quantities, codes, and in general analysis which formulate the evaluation metric of each scheme. Prior to the implementation of the full associative parametric design techniques this would have been done manually and arduously..."[19] He also notes that further automation, optimization and analytical routines were scripted into the design development of the tower as it progressed.

While still a product of its own unique legacy of physical modelmaking, Gehry Partners, with the support of Gehry Technologies, has increased our understanding of the impacts and efficiencies of parametric modeling in integrative architectural design and construction. In the case of tall buildings with their demanding and specific programmatic agendas, these capabilities bring qualitative force to the creative process as well as quantitative force to locating the zones within which design can innovate.

---

[10] Gerber, David, *The Parametric Affect: Computation, Innovation and Models for Design Exploration in Contemporary Architectural Practice,* op. cit.

[11] Schumacher, Patrik, *The Autopoiesis of Architecture,* op. cit.

[12] Deleuze, Gilles, Félix Guattari, *A Thousand Plateaus: Capitalism and Schizophrenia,* op. cit.

[13] Thompson, D'Arcy W., *On Growth and Form,* op. cit.

[14] Mazzoleni, Ilaria, *Architecture Follows Nature-Biomimetic Principles for Innovative Design,* op. cit.

[15] Iwamoto, Lisa, *Digital Fabrications: Architectural and Material Techniques,* op. cit.

[16] Mandelbrot, Benoit, *The Fractal Geometry of Nature,* op cit.

[17] van Berkel, Ben, *Interviews: Raffles City Hangzhou,* http://www.unstudio.com, op. cit.

[18] Castells, Manuel, *The Informational City: Economic Restructuring and Urban Development,* op. cit.

[19] Gerber, David, *The Parametric Affect: Computation, Innovation and Models for Design Exploration in Contemporary Architectural Practice,* op. cit.

CHAPTER FOUR
PERFORMATIVE NEIGHBORHOODS

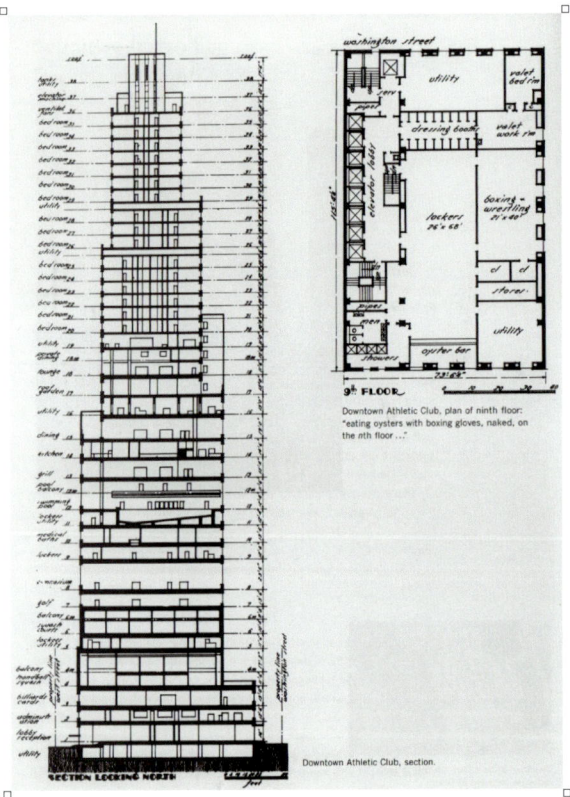

Mile High Tower, unbuilt, 1956 / Frank Lloyd Wright

Downtown Athletic Club, plan of ninth floor: "eating oysters with boxing gloves, naked, on the nth floor ..."

Downtown Athletic Club, section.

Downtown Athletic Club, New York City, 1931 / Starrett and Van Vleck, Duncan Hunter

The idea that tall buildings could one day take mixed-use neighborhoods familiar to us on the horizontal ground plane and string them vertically into the air has always been a compelling vision. Early conceptions, modern and pre-modern, have suggested vivid possibilities. As recounted in TALL BUILDING: IMAGINING THE SKYSCRAPER, turn-of-the-century artwork, and cinema that followed, envisioned a highly dense city of vertical networks carrying transportation systems, retail and amenities skyward. Several early examples were built in Chicago at the end of the 19th century and a number of New York's early and well-known commercial projects including the Waldorf Astoria Hotel, Downtown Athletic Club and Rockefeller Center were noted for their multiple uses from ground level to rooftop. By the late 1930's, visionary proposals by Le Corbusier began to express mixed-uses in the upper floors of his tall buildings as did Frank Lloyd Wright's 1956 proposal for the Mile High Tower also known as The Illinois.

In his long career, Wright actually built only two skyscrapers, ones of modest height: Johnson's Wax Building in Racine, Wisconsin and the Tower in Bartlesville, Oklahoma. By the time he was 89 years old, however, he was proposing a scheme for a 528 floor structure, triangular in shape and 5,280 feet in height. Total rentable area of the tower was to be six million square feet comprising residences, shops, offices and space for concert and recital halls. A tall television antenna crowned the top of the tower with Wright claiming that the transmitter would reach every television set in the United States.

Ironically, the idea of the highly concentrated tower which

John Hancock Center, Chicago, 1970 / Skidmore, Owings & Merrill

would contain a city of up to 100,000 people grew out of Wright's ever-evolving theories of the Prairie House, Broadacre City and his penchant for conserving man's relationship to the ground plane, which he felt would promote independence and democratic health. In retrospect, it is easy to see that Wright's formal rendition of a theoretically mixed-use tower (which gave no expression to the variety within) represented a totemic and simple, if not simplistic, idea. All the internal vitality would, in fact, be subsumed in the overriding symbolism of the supertall icon and the architect's penchant for form.

A similar attitude to form reappeared in 1970 when Skidmore, Owings & Merrill's Bruce Graham and Fazlur Khan completed Chicago's John Hancock Center, one of the first fully realized major mixed-use towers. At 95 stories, the structure was designed to include 700 apartments stacked over 40 floors of office space. Multiple elevator cores serve the office building portion while three cores serve the residential floors. A public observation deck exists on the 94th floor and a restaurant is on the 95th floor. Within the complex are a supermarket, day care center, retail shops, post office, large swimming pool, library and gym. Again, notwithstanding the variety of uses which populate this tower, the formal elements here strongly supported by the structural challenges of building such a tall tower, favor a monolithic exterior form, suppressing the inherent variety within. The exo-skeletal bracing of the skin plus the consistent window-wall conform to a singular building mass. The battered walls and the dropping-off of elevator cores as the building ascends genially accommodates

Shanghai Tower, Shanghai, 2014 / Gensler

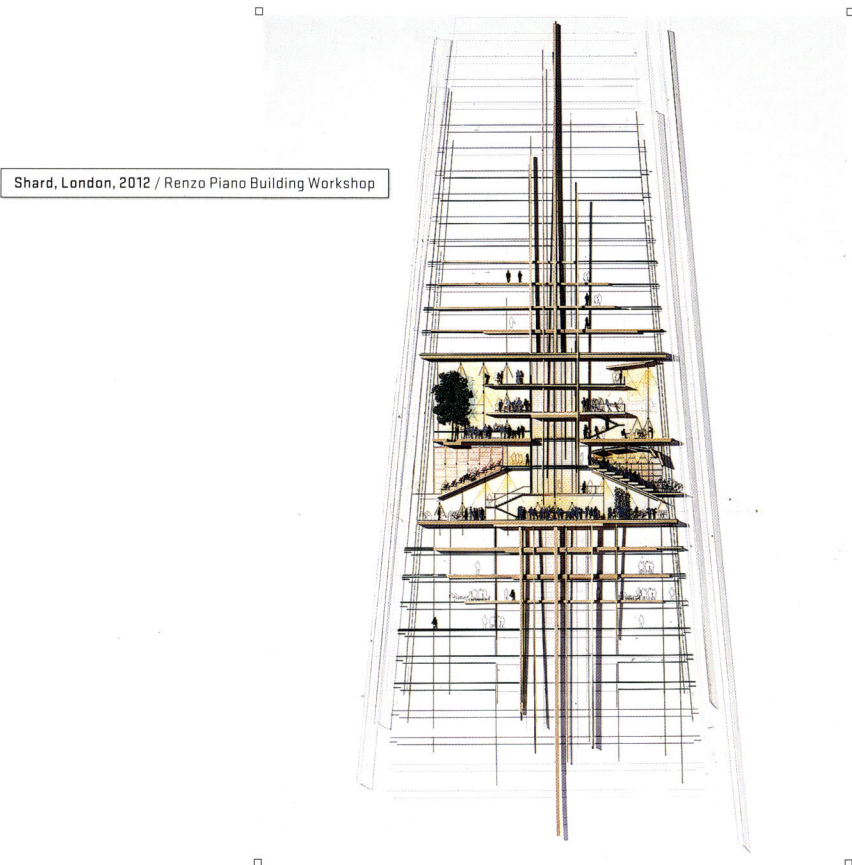

Shard, London, 2012 / Renzo Piano Building Workshop

the change from large office floor requirements below to the more desirable shallow residential floors above.

This tendency toward unified form has continued to the present day in Gensler's Shanghai Tower, fueled by the integration of structural, vertical core and window wall technology and the abiding desire to create iconic imagery in such tall structures. At over 2000 feet in height, the skyscraper will be Pudong's tallest tower, stacking office, hotel, retail and cultural facilities atop one another. Many of the tallest mixed-use buildings in other countries have similarly tended toward unified form such as Renzo Piano's Shard in London and Foster + Partners' proposal for Moscow.

For all the tragedy and labyrinthian follow-up to the events of 9/11 in New York City, the initial presentations to rebuild the neighborhood served to explore a range of new skyscraper typologies. A number of the more memorable ones investigated the prospects for vertical mixed-use communities and horizontal connections between tall buildings. Economic requirements and commercial real estate conventions ultimately weighed down upon the Ground Zero properties and the tall building projects along with conventional briefs were parceled out to a small group of well-recognized international architects. Still, design proposals in the initial rounds, such as those from United Architects, SOM/Sejima & Nishizawa, Meier/Eisenman/Gwathmey/Holl and, later, OMA all showed invention, connectivity and suggested a range of mixed-uses in the upper reaches of the towers.

Among the notable architects who have investigated mixing programs in vertical architecture, Steven Holl is

Russia Tower, Moscow / Foster + Partners

Parallax Towers, New York City, 1990 / Steven Holl Architects

Simmons Hall MIT, Cambridge, 2002 / Steven Holl Architects

perhaps the standout over the past two decades. Beginning with his interconnected Parallax Towers project of 1990, his 2000 extension of the Sarphatistraat Office Building in Amsterdam to Simmons Hall at MIT, Holl has continued to locate opportunities for cross circulation and social/urban spaces within the verticality of the architecture. In Beijing's Linked Hybrid (2009), this trajectory became explicit with a ring of public circulation joining the upper floors of eight residential towers. The Vanke Center in Shenzhen (Horizontal Skyscraper) represent's Holl's continuing effort to elevate mixed-uses, interconnect them horizontally and reduce the footprint of the building at the ground level in favor of landscape and public amenities.

Rem Koolhaus and OMA have worked through a series of projects which attempt to complicate the sheer verticality of tall structures through a kind of unconventional distribution of the building's program and refinements to the vertical circulation systems. The Seattle Library provided an early example of multiple staggered floor plates connected through ramping and elevators within a larger enclosed volume. The idea of the tall building as an extruded stack of typical floor plates was subverted from within and then expressed in its exterior massing and window wall. CCTV took these trends further through a combination of sloping and multiple elevator cores, single individualized floors and large irregular floor plates which connected the two vertical cores. All of this was construed into a non-vertical envelope which again, and more dramatically, subverted the conventional image of the tall building.

Additional investigations of mixed-use architecture in

Linked Hybrid, Beijing, 2008 / Steven Holl Architects

CCTV Headquarters, 2012 / Office for Metropolitan Architecture

Vanke Center, Shenzhen, 2009 / Steven Holl Architects

vertical buildings have come to us from many directions. Theoretical projects from offices as diverse as Adrian Smith/Gordon Gill, MVRDV, BIG and Hans Hollein have explored distinctive ways of enriching the architecture of tall buildings through restructuring their programs and expressing these in form. In other cases, more conventional programming has led to buildings such as Moshe Safdie's Sands SkyPark in Singapore, NRJA's Z Towers in Riga, Latvia and Foster + Partners' Jameson House in Vancouver, all containing a variety of mixed-use elements within an architecture of verticality. Much of the past decade's building boom in the Persian Gulf has yielded interconnected and mixed-use tall buildings from the Dubai Pearl, to the Jeddah Free Trade City in Saudi Arabia.

Finally, the inherent richness of residential programming has given us clues as to the possibilities for mixed-use vertical buildings. Multi-family residential projects like Grimshaw and Dattner Architects' Via Verde in the Bronx often display social activity areas and roof-top amenities throughout their architecture. Unique projects such as Antilia, Mukesh Ambani's 27 story single family residence in Mumbai, while rare, allow us to envision the meaning of vertically connecting highly disparate space-planning typologies.

Ground Zero

Among the most austere and abstract of the entries to the Ground Zero competition was the scheme put forward by the team of Richard Meier, Peter Eisenman, Charles Gwathmey and Steven Holl and their offices. Formally, the project comprised two structures, one with two towers and one with three. Each structure was horizontally connected at upper levels to create the image of three-dimensional super grids. While the drawings, models and renderings were object-like and gave no indication of their contents, the project narrative explained that the proposal combined nine million square feet of office space, a hotel, convention center and unspecified cultural facilities. The multi-story horizontal elements provided structural bracing, enabled horizontal circulation in the upper floors and created super floors for financial trading and convention activities. On the top of each element, sky gardens were planned and the arrangement of compact rectangular floor plates with upper floor connections allowed for the ground plane to be 75 per cent unoccupied and available for landscape and public use.

The New York office of Skidmore, Owings & Merrill assembled a large team of architects, landscape architects and artists to create a project of nine 940 foot tall towers in a large ground plane of reflecting pools. The towers were bent and variously tipping and, on occasion, were joined at the top or at mid-heights. Sixteen acres of sky gardens were planned for the roofs of the towers as well as enclosed gardens within the building masses. Except for the superficial variations of the tower tilts, the towers themselves were virtually undifferentiated and failed to express architecturally the theoretical narrative of vertically mixed-use programs. Public criticism ultimately focused on the undeveloped full-block reflecting pools at the base and the prospective isolation of public parks atop tall buildings. Ultimately SOM withdrew from the competition and elected to continue working instead on 7 World Trade Center which they completed and displays little of the physical vitality or provocations of the early proposal.

As another opportunity to comment on tall buildings, one might expect a clever view of the relationship between history and a radical future from the author of Delirious New York. Rem Koolhaus and OMA employed the idea of the Downtown Athletic Club, an historic wedding-cake building, widely featured in Koolhaus' earlier book, to challenge many of the inherent assumptions of the skyscraper typology. Taking the historic building form and turning it upside-down, the new three-legged tower lands on the ground in a compact footprint maximizing public open space and sunlight. As the three legs rise, they cantilever out to create larger floors and to orient in multiple directions. Ultimately they coalesce toward the top where they become one super-sized floor suitable for larger functions, structurally stabilizing the three legs of the tower and, as it happens, maximizing the amount of commercial space at the top of the building where leasing achieves the highest return. In addition, a new and novel form of elevator circulation is proposed for the building in response to its unique form, elevator cabs which move horizontally as well as vertically. (This feature has been further developed in Beijing's CCTV.) While all this invention constitutes a legitimate challenge to the current tall building typology, the poetry of the scheme is the not-so-subtle suggestion that the historic skyscraper has been turned upside down and driven into the ground, becoming its own tombstone. The death of the skyscraper has, of course, been one of Koolhaus' ongoing pronouncements.

One of the most forward-thinking schemes from the Ground Zero Competition was the proposal from United Architects, a consortium of progressive firms from Amsterdam, London, Los Angeles and New York. While it was designed as five separate towers, this project, more than any other, appeared unified as one large and rambling complex. Each tower grew independently out of the ground level plaza, torquing and leaning toward its companions. Mid-height, these towers merge over many floors, capped by one broad gallery floor connecting all buildings, above which the towers once again separate and rise as independent building tops. While the scheme was one of the most iconic of the entries, it also bisected the Ground Zero neighborhood like a giant wall, limiting visibility and sunlight.

Holl's Vertical Urbanism

Steven Holl has long explored the interconnectivity of complex building sections and in his larger, and taller, buildings; he has attempted to redefine some of the usual assumptions about public and private space. His first building that can be considered tall and in which he aspired to create mixed-use neighborhoods is the student dormitory he designed for MIT known as Simmons Hall. A long slab of a building along the Charles River in Cambridge, the project is long enough to require three elevator cores which allow the architect to articulate the tops of the building as three interconnected but separate towers.

Holl's original vision, exhibited in his early concept sketches, shows that he had hoped for deep sectional cuts in the building from the roof down into the mid-section of the building. These cuts he referred to as "lungs" which would draw sunlight from above down into the bowels of the building, provide spatially interesting visual connections within and allow for natural ventilation of heated air up through these openings. These elements were ultimately cut from the program and the building is left with an array of student lounges scattered throughout the dormitory floors, each of which is expressed on the exterior of the building. Holl sees the building concept as a kind of "sponge" which is porous and allows common space to be embedded and display itself within the outward expression of the building.

This seemingly organic concept recalls some of the recent work of Toyo Ito, his studies for the Belgian Cultural Center in Ghent and his new Opera House in Taichung City, Taiwan.

A few years later and opening in time for the 2008 Beijing Olympics, the cluster of eight residential towers known as the Linked Hybrid opened adjacent to the site of the old city wall, displaying many of the same investigations taken now to a larger and more vertical scale. Because the towers are each separate in space, a level of hybridization and connectivity is achieved by the inclusion of a series of upper-level bridges which connect all towers and create a circulation circuit throughout. The ground plane is reserved for common space, landscape, water features, plazas and elevator lobbies, however the idea of public services and, prospectively, cultural and retail opportunities, was imagined for these long upper-level galleries and bridges. This vision recalls Le Corbusier's plans over a half century ago for the Unite de Habitation wherein he proposed a retail street in the mid-section of the residential tower. Just as Le Corbusier's plan was ultimately unfulfilled, so has Holl's efforts to create public opportunities in the upper register of the towers remained largely unfulfilled. To date, apartment tower life at the Linked Hybrid still appears to be a generally private existence with public interaction drawn more to the landscape and out-of-doors of the ground level where residents arrive and depart.

Sliced Porosity Block at the First Ring Road and Ren Min Nan Road in Chengdu represents Holl's continuing exploration of infusing access and public space, in a word, "porosity," into a monumental building project where most of the vertical program is clearly fixed and, to a large extent, typological. Using China's highly restrictive sun/shadow codes as a departure point, Holl has oriented and sliced the five towers to admit maximum natural light into the resulting public spaces and the project's urban neighborhood. In an attempt to foil the conventional retail podium, Holl has created an elaborate water landscape at the roof of the six story shopping center, turned stores outside to the ground level sidewalk and brought stairs, ramps and landscape elements down off the roof to grade. Above the three-pond plaza rise the five towers, oblique and rotated yet containing typical programs of office space, serviced apartments and hotel.

Holl's Vanke Center in Shenzhen is the most extreme

Sliced Porosity Block - CapitaLand Raffles City Chengdu, Chengdu, 2012 / Steven Holl Architects

Sliced Porosity Block - CapitaLand Raffles City Chengdu, Chengdu, 2012 / Steven Holl Architects

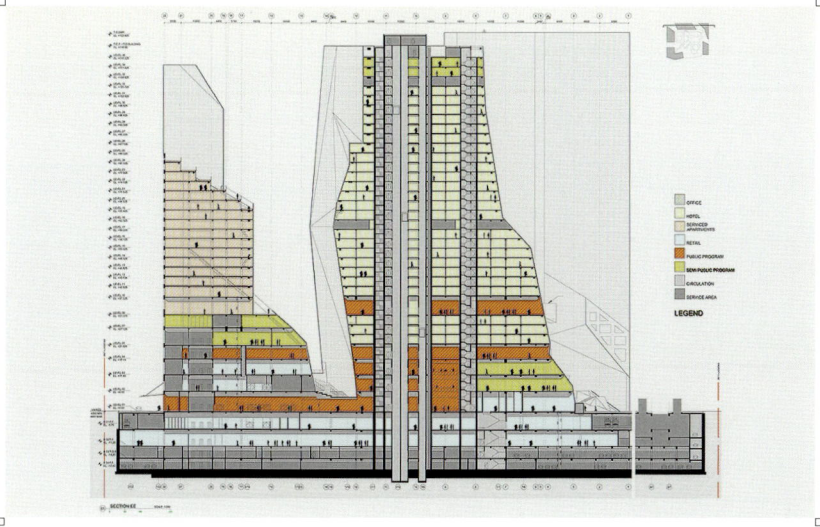

Matrix Gateway Complex, Proposal, Dubai, 2010 / Adrian Smith + Gordon Gill

example of what can happen by commingling mixed-use programs above grade. While not truly a vertical tower, the project, often referred to as The Horizontal Skyscraper, divides 1.2 million square feet of enclosed space horizontally into office, hotel and apartments, lifting these programs above the ground level, connected only by vertical circulation. This opens up the vast majority of the ground plane to elaborate social spaces, recreation and landscape. Further, it draws the clearest possible distinction between architecture and the architect's vision of nature.

Monoliths
In 2010, Adrian Smith + Gordon Gill Architecture produced a conceptual plan for a monolithic building in the shape of a giant gridded cube. This cube was a massive 180 meters in each direction built on an 18 meter steel super-grid. Within the grid, 5 vertical cores serviced a variety of uses including office, hotel and conference facilities, residential, recreation, cultural programs and a prayer hall. These uses were proposed to interact with each other, have their own circulation cores and look into each other much as a dense city does within the overall framework of the cube. The cube was planned to sit on a waterfront marina in Dubai accessible by boat, automobiles and a helipad. Parking constituted the lower portions of the cube.

In the context of the Gulf Coast, the semi-transparent skin covering the cube is embedded with shading screens and solar panels which reduce solar gain while generating electricity for the complex. The condensate from the

Sky Village, Rodovre, 2008 / MVRD / ADEPT

humidity in the air is collected and converted into drinking water. Water from the gulf will cool the complex as will interior waterfalls and the breeze which penetrates its open skin.

The elegance of the scheme is its radical inversion of a building's exterior. Once the cube exterior has been conceived, both the form of the complex and the central environmental features are established. Thereafter, the mixed-use program elements are free to interact with each other internally. While views to the exterior are now protected and shaded, interior spaces are infinitely flexible and create a new kind of "tall building volume" which heightens the importance of the spaces between building programs as much as it allows flexibility for the building programs themselves.

Stacked Cells

In 2008, the municipality of Rodovre, an independent community in Copenhagen, announced MVRDV and ADEPT as winners of a design competition for the Rodovre Skyscraper. The 116 meter tall tower accommodates apartments, a hotel, retail and offices. The lower levels of the tower provides space for retail and restaurants within a surrounding public plaza. The design concept is unique in at least three ways.

First, the tower typology is conceptualized as a central vertical core which provides structural support as well as bustles together the several and separate circulation and mechanical cores servicing each of the different stacked uses in the tower. Around this wide core are cantilevered a series of flexible cellular units which

56 Leonard Street, New York City, 2015 / Herzog & de Meuron

are modular and can be adapted to the apartment, hotel and office planning modules.

Second, because of this cellular conception, the mass of occupied space can be "sculpted" through a process of repositioning the cells depending upon use, orientation and desired floor plate configuration. In that way, the building is narrow at its base, maximizing landscaped open space, and begins to widen for office space above. On top of the office space, the cells begin to lean to the north which creates steps, or terraces, on the sunnier south side of the building. At the top, the hotel guest rooms are located with the most commanding views and set back only where personal outdoor spaces are matched to suites.

Finally, and conceptually, the project proposes to fuse the notion of a single family home with the conventionally monolithic skyscraper typology. The Sky Village, as the architects refer to the tower, recalls the efforts of Metabolists of the 1960s and 70s and the Field Theorists of the same period. Specifically, Moshe Safdie's Habitat in Montreal and Kisho Kurokawa's Capsule Building in Tokyo's Ginza are recalled as is the more recent 56 Leonard in New York City by Herzog & de Meuron.

Sandwiches

Recently, Atelier Hollein made public its proposal for the SBF Tower in Shenzhen, China. The project is sited adjacent to the Town Hall on its north-south axis and is in a central position on Shen Nan Avenue in the Central Business District. The design is based upon a sketch Hans Hollein made years ago during his time in Chicago when,

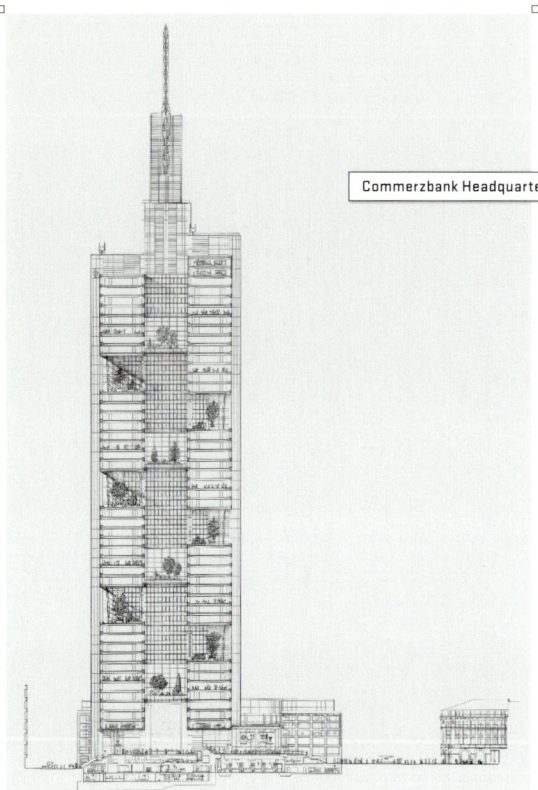

Commerzbank Headquarters, Frankfurt, 1997 / Foster + Partners

Yongsan International Business District, "Project R6," Planned Completion 2016 / REX

reacting to the city's architectural legacy, he was theorizing tall buildings of the future. The scheme proposes a strong dialectic between the banality of rectangular office tower conventions and the possibility for unrestrained flexibility in designated zones within the larger typology. At 42 floors in height and a total area of approximately one million square feet, the tower's design is based upon a 45 meter square plan surrounding a square vertical circulation and engineering core. Four stacks of six levels of conventional office space are separated vertically by the equivalent of five floors of sky gardens, amenities and creative workplace environments. The project attempts to capture a wider range of the working population and bring support uses normally found on the ground plane up into the shaft of the tower. Reminiscent of Foster + Partners Commerzbank Headquarters in Frankfurt and more restrained yet reminiscent of Ken Yeang's efforts to bring variety and landscape materials into the body of the building, the SBF Tower presents similar ideas with a clarity that improvises without disrupting the tall office building paradigm.

Towers and Bars

Two tower projects proposed by young architects illustrate some of the issues which concern the insertion of a defined horizontal space into the midsection of a conventional tower typology. Bjarke Ingels and BIG have designed the Cross # Towers, adjacent to Studio Liebeskind's Yongsan Master Plan in Seoul, Korea. The building design involves two very conventional-appearing residential towers connected by 2 horizontal bars of residential units and amenities plus another

Yongsan International Business District, Cross # Towers, Seoul / BIG

8 House, Orestad, 2010 / BIG

horizontal connection in the basement of the project. One imagines that the bars are accessed by way of horizontal circulation systems connecting the two vertical cores at the center of each of the towers. We are told that the bars are pierced with interior atria ringed with amenities such as libraries, gallery space and a kindergarten. The rooftops of the bars are shown to provide long open spaces for recreational use. The building skins, while conventional in elevation, are developed in profile to respond to their different solar orientations.

Museum Plaza, a 62 story multi-tower scheme in Louisville, Kentucky by REX architects explores similar relationships. A mixed-use program is devised as a commercial method for supporting non-profit entities, namely, a contemporary art institute and university Master of Fine Arts program. The cultural program is a three story element which is positioned at the 24th floor, with 98 luxury condos and 270,000 square feet of office space above, a 250-room Westin hotel and 117 loft apartments below. Inside the cultural element at mid-span are retail, gym, restaurants and social spaces for the building occupants. This horizontal element is referred to by the architects as "the island" and their hope is to co-mingle these social and cultural amenities within the verticality of the project, freeing up the ground plane for a large-scale open plaza.

Other Strategies

BIG, the eponymous firm of Bjarke Ingels, has been experimenting with vertical buildings which reinterpret hybrid three-dimensional form. In the case of its first major building, 8 House, seven miles from the city center of Copenhagen, BIG has produced a mixed-use residential building which includes 476 apartments and more than 100,000 square feet of commercial and shared space. The configuration of the building is such that it ascends from the ground plane at one corner and creates a green promenade which runs atop a figure-eight roof slab and encircles two ground level courtyards. Residential units which set back allow for large terraces as well as a green garden and exercise trail which circumnavigates the entire building by way of its roof tops.

This idea of merging hybrid verticality with traditional courtyards reappears in BIG's proposal for West 57, a 457 foot tall sloping tower which includes 600 apartments and 130,000 square feet of cultural and commercial space at the ground level. The scheme achieves considerable vertical density while preserving a private and secure ground level courtyard for residents. The current planning approval process is focusing on the exclusively private use of open space and the question of whether to provide neighborhood retail at the street level in an area of Hell's Kitchen which one day may be more heavily populated but today is spotty and industrial in character.

Finally, Ingels' proposal for Beach and Howe, a 49 story mixed-use residential tower proposed for one of 3 triangular sites in Vancouver employs similar hybrid form, this time, resolutely vertical, to maximize density over an oblique site and limit shade and shadow on adjacent properties. Nine floors at the base of the tower will accommodate offices, retail shops and restaurants and will spill out to form a series of public plazas beneath an adjacent elevated highway.

Other design strategies which have the effect of horizontally connecting vertical space and stem from early prototypes such as Pelli's Petronas Towers include NRJA's twin tower project, Z Towers, in Riga, Latvia. Multiple floors become bridges between towers providing connections between vertical cores and natural locations for common space and amenities to be shared by tower occupants. Comparable strategies include the top floor in projects such as Schweger Associated Architects' Dubai Pearl, four towers connected laterally at the roof. Moshe Safdie's Marina Bay Sands in Singapore unites three atria hotel towers at the base, connects with an Expo and Convention Center and at the top with a SkyPark which includes recreational and retail amenities.

Individuality and Expression

Among the most visionary, and perhaps for practical reasons, the most promising prospects for radicalizing the mixed-use tall building are those proposals which express the deep programmatic variety which can exist within a tall building's envelope. These proposals are usually promoted as a way to overcome the repetitive and generic skins which mask the variety within and may limit the range of interior/exterior relationships a tall building can provide to inhabitants. While conventional skins and shapes may seem indifferent, they frequently provide a neutrality which gives them a measure of adaptability over time. Contrarily, when a tall building is built at relatively great expense, to the degree that its configuration and exterior wall are highly customized, then those same conditions likely impose their own constraints to change in the future. No one can yet explain how modifications on the 47th floor, for example, to the shell and core of a tall residential building and its impact on its neighbors would be as minimal as the modifications to a one or two-story single-family house and its neighborhood impact. However, as building systems evolve and residential and work patterns change, these plug-in plans may become viable.

Vertical Neighborhood, a mixed-use tower for 53 West 53rd (MoMA Tower) by Axis Mundi with modeling by Live Architecture Network (LaN) is such a proposal. John Beckmann, the architect, states that..."historically, the skyscraper was a unitary, homogeneous form that reflected the generic, flexible office space it contained... The Vertical Neighborhood is more organic and more flexible an assemblage of disparate architectural languages. It reflects an emerging reality for tall buildings as post-boom era, expressing the diversity of uses within instead of one-note architecture that makes a singular visual image and little else."[20] Beckmann's tower recalls the realities of Le Corbusier's first major housing project in Pessac on the outskirts of Bordeaux. Fifty homes designed and built in an austere Modern style in 1926 later received shutters, flower pots, sloping tile roofs and decorated exteriors as residents changed and new arrivals personalized their dwellings. While the Vertical Neighborhood proposal is based on a formulaic stacking system, it appears to accommodate diversity and self-expression.

West 57, New York City, Planned Completion 2015 / BIG

Beach and Howe, Vancouver / BIG

Marina Bay Sands Resort, Singapore, 2011 / Moshe Safdie Architects

Vertical Neighborhood, Proposal, New York City, 2009 / Axis Mundi

Antilia Towers, Mumbai, 2010 / Perkins + Will

The constructive system involves two central vertical cores which carry services and circulation. Wrapped around those two cores, with some flexibility, are a series of what the architects call "Smart Blocks," comprising 2 story rings of modular spatial envelopes which can be inserted into the mass of the tower with considerable variety. Spatial voids may occur between blocks, providing access for light and air and exterior private space. In addition to the bold narrative, The Vertical Neighborhood proposes to replace Jean Nouvel's Tower Verre, an 82-story hotel/condo/art gallery tower affiliated with the museum. Thirty stories lesser in height, the "Neighborhood" carries the visual animation of the street level up the full height of the tower.

This kind of natural variety is most frequently found in residential projects. Commercial office towers seem inherently designed for speculation and generalized occupancies while contemporary hotels are principally a vertical collection of stacked guest rooms whose features from bathrooms to window-lines are generally repetitive. Their success in the hospitality marketplace seems more dependent on the amenitization of the interior than on the aesthetic properties of the building envelope. The recent opening of Via Verde, the 222 unit apartment complex for low and middle income households in the South Bronx illustrates the kinds of generators of form which can articulate the exterior of a residential program. This project which is anchored by a 20-story tower on one end and steps down to grade with a series of highly activated terraces, is a collaborative effort of Grimshaw, Dattner Architects and the Jonathan Rose Companies. A medical clinic is located at the ground floor with staggered terraces encompassing orchards, food gardens, and recreational decks above. A seventh floor fitness center overlooks one of the green roofs, a laundry room faces a courtyard play area, allowing parents to watch their children while a community room occupies the top floor adjacent to an outdoor terrace for social events and meetings. All this specific programming in the building concept results in specific design cues which animate the architecture.

Finally, while perhaps not a typology easily or often imitated, Mumbai's Antilia Tower by Robert Goodwin of the New York Office of Perkins + Will and HBA expresses the results of a highly specific and personalized residential program for one family. Designed and built for Mukesh Ambani, reputedly India's richest industrialist, and his family of six, the Tower is 27 floors tall and comprises 400,000 square feet. Including a parking structure for 168 autos and 3 helipads, the "house" combines conventional domestic spaces with fitness center, 3 indoor swimming pools, yoga and dance studios and a 50 seat cinema. The tower residence reportedly runs on a staff of 600. Without regard to the social and cultural implications of this particular tower, it gives vision to the prospect for a vertical building which effusively displays the variety of its contents.

[20] *Axis Mundi Unveils Conceptual Design for MoMA Tower, Designboom.com.* Designboom.com, op. cit.

CHAPTER FIVE
PERFORMATIVE CITIES

For over 5000 years scattered peoples have been migrating to cities with the aspiration of finding security, work and prosperity. While hopes have not always been fulfilled, the city has continued to grow as earth's primary urban form. In the 20th century, global urban growth had increased so precipitously that by 2006, the United Nations estimated that half of the world population lived in cities. By 2050, it has been estimated that 75 per cent of the population will occupy cities.

Historically, we know that a disproportionately large amount of a country's wealth is generated in cities. When a major city's economic strength begins to wane, and that strength migrates to more attractive cities, the well-being of nation-states is affected. Mega cities of several million people as well as larger metropolitan conurbations follow paths of industrialization and employment opportunities and attempt to capture wealth. In today's international marketplace, cities fight for global competitiveness in order to insure jobs, municipal funds for housing, transit and public infrastructure and a generally improved quality of life. Transnational trade and travel patterns affect the vitality and ultimately the physical manifestation of each city.

In addition to economic forces, social, political and cultural patterns impact the nature of each city's growth. In the past decade and a half, London has become one of the world's great financial capitals, experiencing a renewed wave of growth and tourism. As a result, it has become necessary for the city to reorganize and embrace additional density, taller buildings and new housing stock in order to accommodate international business and the nearly one million new residents expected in the next decade.

The entire Japanese archipelago functions as one interdependent urban entity due to the fact that its capital, Tokyo, can be reached from virtually anywhere in a matter of a few hours due to its sophisticated network of high-speed trains. Conversely, while eighty per cent of the Japanese population uses public transport to get to work, eighty per cent of Angelenos use private automobiles. While sixty per cent of all residents in Mexico City live in unregistered and illegal housing, the city government of Shanghai is rushing to provide more office space and vertical housing for workers moving to the city. Twenty-five years ago, there were fewer than 300 buildings over ten stories in height. Today there are nearly 3,000.

While many factors account for the stark differences among the world's largest cities, the disproportionate levels of natural resources these cities consume create disproportionate environmental impacts. In developed countries, it is estimated that nearly half of their energy budgets are spent on buildings with an additional quarter on transportation. While cities appear to be both inevitable and on the rise, their current environmental costs are enormous.

It is against this backdrop of global diversity and caution that our final essay looks at the PERFORMATIVE SKYSCRAPER in its physical and cultural context. How can the concept of performativity be relevant to the morphology of cities and their relationship to skyscrapers? In this chapter, and in the broadest sense of the term, we examine how individual skyscrapers have evolved to perform in the context of a number of major cities. While we understand the history of the skyscraper to be the product of growing urbanization, increased density, rising land values and the technologies that enable verticality, each major city defines what is possible in its own terms. It is compelling to imagine a singular skyscraper type resulting from the now shared means and methods of a culture of international designers and builders. Nonetheless, climatic conditions, history and culture, socio-demographic events and the intersection of local politics and capital investment all act to create unique skyscrapers in unique cities.

New York City

The city of New York covers approximately 300 square miles of which twenty-five per cent is dedicated to open space. The gross residential density of New York City is about 27,000 residents per square mile, by far the highest in the United States, however, residential densities within the city are unevenly distributed and vary widely from peaks in parts of Manhattan to the relative low densities of areas in the outer boroughs with a notably suburban character. With a Gross City Product of approximately $65,000 per capita, New York is one of the world's richest cities, generating nearly four percent of the United States economy. The city's employment profile is thoroughly post-industrial. More than ninety percent of adult New Yorkers have a job or work freelance in the services and business sector.

New York City is the original City of Skyscrapers. Putting

aside the claims between Chicago and New York for the actual birthplace of the building type, New York quickly took the lead in becoming a city physically characterized by the conflation of outsized real estate ambition and advanced building technology in the form of the ubiquitous skyscraper. The city's first skyscrapers appeared in the dense commercial neighborhoods of Lower Manhattan, frequently small and eccentric in shape due to the constraints of the original Dutch street plan. As Carol Willis, Columbia University professor and Director of the Skyscraper Museum, has recounted, Cass Gilbert's Woolworth tower reached 790 feet in height, breaking the earlier 400 foot record by almost double. The 1931 Empire State Building rose to 1,250 feet and was the city's, and world's, tallest building until it was surpassed by the World Trade Center in 1973. New York then immediately passed the mantle of "world's tallest" to Chicago's Sears Tower in 1974.

Manhattan's unique contribution to the skyscraper has been three-fold. First, owing to its extreme density and broad commercialization, the total number of high-rise buildings and their aggregate area has created an urban context which is pre-eminently vertical with both predictable and unforeseen consequences.

Second, due to the great number of tall buildings which have been built and the relatively high degree of design experimentation which has occurred over time, major high-rise trends have been absorbed into the city's zoning ordinances, restricting skyscraper trends in some cases and extending the lives of others for decades. This is apparent to historians of the building type. The years in which the zoning code has been fundamentally rewritten to accommodate new perceptions of the skyscraper are well-known: 1916, 1961, 1982 and the current period in which constraints as to height limits and density are once again being redrawn.

Third, looking over the roster of public events which promote conversation about the idea of the skyscraper, one would have to consider the events of 9/11 and the attempts to rebuild Ground Zero as a watershed moment in the public's consideration of future possibilities for the building type. The multiple narratives of fear and ambition, the symbolic value of extreme height, the confirmation that private structures act as public icons, and the breathtaking domination of politics and commerce in ultimately controlling the capitalization of new skyscrapers, all defined the contemporary skyscraper in the public mind.

New York, as the early modern metropolis, had been built on coal and steam power, fed by railways and supplied by ships sailing into its harbor. While the city lacked the grand boulevards and public spaces of European capitals, it enjoyed a rigorous street grid north of downtown which organized building parcels, identified locations for neighborhood parks and fostered modest circulation throughout the city. As inexpensive petroleum fed the burgeoning automobile industry, this same street grid failed to accommodate increasingly dense traffic. Robert Moses, Chairman of the Triborough Bridge and Tunnel Authority attempted to develop major elevated highways through the city while proposing inner-city urban renewal plans based upon the Corbusian model of segregation: dense vertical populations, open ground planes and isolated cross-town highways. Fortunately, Moses was never successful in his most extreme visions for Manhattan although many of his strategies were ultimately built out in other American cities.

In contrast to Moses, the Rockefeller family, following the development of Rockefeller Center, continued to build large urban complexes within the city's existing grid. They donated the land for the United Nations and built the first skyscraper in Lower Manhattan since the Depression, the Chase Manhattan Bank building (1961) designed by Skidmore, Owings & Merrill's Gordon Bunshaft. Both these institutions had timely global implications, the UN in terms of establishing United States, and New York, centrality in world politics and diplomacy, the Chase Manhattan Bank in terms of a similar presence in world finance and global trade. Research under the auspices of the New York Regional Plan Association (RPA) and supported by the Rockefeller Brothers Fund recommended that New York should de-emphasize manufacturing and trade and in their place, plan for a future in finance, insurance and real estate development. New York City, "the capital of capital" at mid-twentieth century, was already consolidating its position as a global service center with real estate as its corollary asset. The modern skyscraper was the physical embodiment of both. Less than a decade later, the Rockefellers were sponsors of the World Trade Center, near the Chase Manhattan Bank and containing over 10 million square feet of commercial

New York City Skyline

space in one project in the world's two tallest buildings.

Partly due to its planning and foresight, New York City has, over the long term, withstood the powerful shocks of de-industrialization. The fiscal crisis of the late 1970s was brought on by economic recession, declining tax revenues and increasing expenditures owing, in part, to an expansion of social programs. Throughout the 1980s, the city hemorrhaged industrial companies and jobs, causing it to lose its position as the country's largest manufacturing center. In 1987, the stock-market bust, and the real estate recession which followed, sent another blow to building investment in the city. In the late 1990s, the dot.com implosion struck and again, in 2008, the global financial crash followed by recession challenged New York's ability to move forward.

As the premier financial capital in the US, New York has been both susceptible to market shifts even as it has benefitted from predominance in many of those markets over the long term. Historically, one of a very few global financial centers, it continues to generate economic activity in this sector in Lower Manhattan and the New York regional market. As the home of the United Nations, New York enjoys considerable capital expenditure due to the presence of the international community. With regard to media, the major broadcast television networks and many cable networks are headquartered within the city as are some of the country's predominant arts institutions. Major museums, dance companies and theater, including Broadway, generate sizeable economic activity and promote global tourism. These venues plus the many institutions of higher education and elite medical centers sustain a vast non-profit sector.

The city dominates domestic markets in the fields of fashion, artistic and literary production, and multimedia design. Finally, it should be mentioned that, since the 1980s, New York City has experienced the continual influx of hundreds of thousands of immigrants who both contribute to economic activity and generate foreign visitation.

The Mayor of New York has the ability to exercise considerable authority as it relates to zoning and the structuring of public/private participation in major building projects. Actions of the Economic Development Corporation (EDC), a semi-autonomous mayoral agency, undergo local reviews and approval but frequently the EDC operates in conjunction with the Empire State Development Corporation, which, as an agency of state government, is immune from regulations requiring normal citizen participation. The EDC's efforts have resulted in a string of large mixed-use projects including both high-rise buildings and ground-level amenities from Battery Park City, Brooklyn's MetroTech, the Times Square Redevelopment Project, midtown's Columbus Circle development and the Hudson Yards. Mayor Bloomberg has encouraged denser high-rise construction in formerly industrial neighborhoods, larger projects on the Far West Side of Manhattan, Long Island City, Queens and waterfront redevelopment on the Manhattan side of the East River and in Brooklyn.

In 2007, Bloomberg announced a plan to accommodate population growth through the year 2030. Targeting the construction of 265,000 new housing units, he proposed re-zoning to allow increased densities, more market-rate housing and the subsidies for affordable and low-income housing. In his last term, he identified a 70-block area around Grand Central Terminal newly-called Midtown East for additional density and unrestricted heights. His goal has been to re-establish a premier office location for the next generation of high-rise commercial buildings. Already, two important residential buildings are underway at over 90 stories in height. Provisions in the proposed zoning would allow real estate developers to pay the city an unspecified amount for a "district improvement bonus" in exchange for an additional 20 per cent density bonus. Additional density could be achieved through air rights transfer from nearby historic landmarks or from the city.

While skyscrapers may be the visual symbols of commercial and economic success, they can also be the cause of other invasive conditions which limit quality of life in the dense post-industrial city. Such densities as those realized in high-rise Manhattan, require extensive public transportation systems in order to adequately service such neighborhoods. New York City's Metropolitan Transportation Authority provides for more than half of all daily journeys conducted in the city each day. The fiscal resources needed to keep this service up-to-date are massive and the task of running the system as an acceptably safe, efficient and attractive transport option is forever challenging. Just meeting the financial obligations of bond issues made to fund large ongoing investments in transport infrastructure requires ongoing political action and financial planning. Additionally, impact tolls for auto traffic in Lower Manhattan and the ever-expanding bicycle programs from the creation of dedicated lanes to the ambitious CitiBike rentals represent public attempts to provide alternative transportation modes to the private automobile.

As the city's planning efforts have focused on stimulating economic expansion and residential construction, the costs of developing dense, more vertical building structures has had the effect of raising price points, causing a crisis in affordable housing. This has been exacerbated in a recessionary economy causing an out-migration of middle and working class families to the suburbs.

Following the historic and visionary example of the construction of Central Park, New York appears to have understood well the important relationship between public open space and the increasing densification and verticality of the modern city. In recent years, the city has promoted and found inventive ways to fund a wide array of public space improvements from the further development of Battery Park and the Westside Highway to the East River Park system, Brooklyn Bridge Park, Governors Island Park, Ellis Island, the High Line and Fresh Kills Park on Staten Island. As much of New York's waterfront has de-industrialized, the city has rezoned this land to residential use while preserving public access. New housing projects are being developed, much of them high-end. As a result, speculative land purchases are stimulating price inflation.

Historically, New York City mayors have exercised their broad discretionary powers to create private investment opportunities in order to pay for public infrastructure. The recent Bloomberg administration was known to expand those opportunities into all five boroughs, blending speculative real estate projects with proposed public amenities. These opportunities have typically been structured to provide height and density bonuses, tax subsidies and/or land contributions to private developers. Public policy experts vary in opinion as to whether this cost/benefit quid-pro-quo actually expands urban economic development or whether the enterprise is a zero sum game, gentrifying select neighborhoods while relocating lower-utilization land use and less affluent communities to new outlying areas. In either case, Mayor de Blasio inherits an aggressive high-rise, high-density plnning effort.

London

Greater London covers approximately 620 square miles of land area and a population of some 7.5 million residents. The metropolitan area has a relatively low residential density of 11,400 residents per square mile and almost half of its surface is comprised of open and recreational space. Approximately twenty-seven per cent of the city's current population was born outside the United Kingdom and over ninety per cent of residential migration into the city in the past decade are from non-natives. With its service-led economy, London is considered one of the world's most expensive cities and registers a Gross City Product estimated at $55,000 per capita, amounting to 20 per cent of the United Kingdom's national economy. Although known as one of the world's great financial centers, London's creative industries, including advertising, media, fashion and design, now, surprisingly, provide more jobs than financial services.

Born of a network of small urban villages, London never had a City Plan per se. Even today, villages such as Hampstead, Chelsea, Greenwich, Chiswick, Stratford, Stoke Newington and Wimbledon are still distinctly defined communities within the larger polycentric city. Christopher Wren's rushed attempts to lay out London in a grand baroque style following the Great Fire of 1666 failed and the city was immediately rebuilt. Only the Green Belt, Patrick Abercrombie's planning policy implemented as a part of the 1943 Greater London Plan, has survived.

Frequently referred to as the "ungovernable city," London's political structure is fragmented into 33 boroughs within the boundaries of the Greater London Authority (GLA) overseen by an executive mayor. By contrast, New York City, with a similar population size, occupies half the footprint of London, yet is made up of only five boroughs controlled by a mayor with strong executive powers. Like New York, London sits within a larger regional megalopolis encompassing 19 million people, spreading primarily into the southeast of England, many of whom commute to London daily.

To understand London's peculiar background as a city with both a tradition of grand open spaces as well as one with consistently low-rise, low-density character, it is important to know that large sections of the city are defined by the eighteenth and nineteenth-century estates of great aristocratic families, emanating from the Stuart and Hanoverian monarchies. Large parts of London's most valuable real estate remain in the hands of aristocratic estates, the Bedford Estate, the Grosvenor Estate and the Queen's own Crown Estate. These cover some of the city's most elegant streets and squares, many of them surrounded by white-stuccoed townhouses. An aerial view of London reveals this peculiar and organic urban structure. Acres of two and three story terraced housing stretch outward from the city center for more than 20 miles in all directions.

In the wake of World War II and thereafter, London followed a policy of relatively low-rise reconstruction and redevelopment when compared to other world capitals such as New York or Tokyo. The city's traditional policy of opposing tall buildings has been the result of many factors: its historically low-rise character, a desire to protect view corridors to landmark structures such as St. Paul's Cathedral and Westminster Cathedral, and a concern for fire and life safety in tall buildings rooted in tragic events in public housing from the 1960s. Add to that the aforementioned fragmentary city governance system and an expansive physical geography which allowed the city to spread out rather than densify, and skyscrapers were seldom built. The first serious examples of densification and a tall building district were at Canary Wharf, a part of the larger docklands redevelopment efforts targeted by the City at a major brownfield site on the east side of London. The site was far away from historic buildings and views.

These first tall building efforts began as part of an urban

London Skyline

regeneration strategy to combat urban ills many major western cities were confronting in the 1970s, namely, de-industrialization, structural unemployment and the inner-city decline that followed. The conservative economic policies of Margaret Thatcher's government, particularly between 1979 and 1987, accelerated the economic and social decline affecting British cities. Subsidies were withdrawn from declining industries such as coal-mining, steel and auto production, leading to a rise in unemployment and reduced economic activity throughout the United Kingdom. Realizing that intervention would be required to revive the economies of areas where old industries had disappeared, development corporations were set up in the dockland areas and tax breaks were given to businesses in these newly designated "enterprise zones."

London's population, which had reached over 8.5 million in the 1940s, dropped to 6.7 million by 1986. City docks and industrial areas were abandoned and a growing divide between the affluent suburbs and the urban poor loomed. Civil unrest broke out in many neighborhoods and appeared to parallel the events of American inner cities surrounded by "white flight" edge communities. Rapid deceleration in a country of historically broad social-democratic traditions led to a series of policy responses at both the national and local levels. Politically, Canary Wharf and the development of docklands properties became, in part, a visible symbol of such reinvestment.

The creation of a London mayoralty in 2000 marked the opening of a great debate about many things, including the appropriateness of tall buildings in the city. The new "executive mayor," Ken Livingstone, and his assembly of twenty-five, became responsible for most transportation and economic development in the city. The mayor was required to publish a spatial-development strategy, which became known as the "London Plan." Livingstone used this plan to increase density in urban areas and to encourage the use of public transportation as a strategy for the reduction of fossil fuel consumption. The mayor also planned to shift development of the city from the west to the underdeveloped and impoverished east, most notably through his decision to locate the 2012 Olympic Games in east London.

While Livingstone recognized the historic sensitivity of protected views to landmarks, he insisted that new high-rise construction could complement, rather than conflict with, the historic London cityscape. To that end, he mobilized London-specific research to build a case for a tall buildings agenda. He took the position that "For London to remain a competitive world city, it must respond to the drivers of growth and continue to develop in a dynamic, organic, manner without inappropriate restraints."[21] Livingstone noted that the population in London was once again on the rise, its position as a global financial center amid a booming economy was visible and immigrants were becoming residents in huge numbers. According to Livingstone's London Plan, for the city to remain competitive at the global scale, it needed to accommodate up to 600,000 new jobs and 400,000 new households by the year 2016. The British Council for Offices predicted considerable growth in office space over the following 25 years while commercial boosters outlined familiar rationale: density would maximize profitability, construction investment would stimulate other aspects of the larger economy and the clustering of tall buildings would elevate footfall, sales and real estate values as well as promote productivity and energy efficiency.

Livingston's vision for a modern-day London was suffused with his personal desire for a dramatic and definable skyline like those of Shanghai and Manhattan. London's new mayoralty government was the key to enabling this vision. New towers began to breach the 305 meter limit along Bishopsgate and tall building proposals displayed unique silhouettes and skins. In less than a decade, London went from an ungovernable city to one with a strong vision which included skyscrapers, increasing the city's density and providing symbols of national financial prowess. This recent burst of policy recalled earlier periods when London had served as a transportable urban model. John Nash's early 19th century plan for London was sufficiently heroic to inspire Napoleon III to remodel Paris just as the London Underground later set the standard for the creation of the Paris Metro. The Barbican, London Wall and Paternoster Square were all the results of policy and planning strategies which were copied in other world cities.

Once again, the population of London is growing, immigration is up and the city is becoming more central to economic activity in Europe and the Middle East. The current mayor, Boris Johnson, has largely continued the pro-development and construction program of his predecessor. Updating the London Plan in 2011, he has attempted to bolster the technology sector, commercial office construction and extended Enterprise Zones in the Docklands. At the same time, the Plan is largely governed by the London View Management Framework which attempts to protect view corridors to historic sites, a subject of great public interest since the original tall building construction that followed World War II.

Paris
Paris is the capital and largest city in France. With a population of approximately 2.2 million and a metropolitan area of 40 square miles surrounded by the Boulevard Peripherique, it is one of the largest population centers in Europe. At 55,000 inhabitants per square mile, excluding the large woodland parks of Boulogne and Vincennes, Paris is one of the most densely populated cities in the world, comparable only to certain Asian cities and the borough of Manhattan. While the city was founded over 2000 years ago, by the 12th century, Paris was one of Europe's most important cultural centers and the largest Western European city until the 18th century. The city population reached its historic peak of 2.9 million in 1921 and since then has declined much like other Western cities that have experienced a reduction in household size and a outward migration to suburban areas. One of the most multi-cultural cities in Europe, 20 per cent of Paris' total population was born outside France. Since the 1970's, familiar issues of de-industrialization and gentrification in the urban core have been a part of life in Paris.

Notwithstanding its considerable density, Paris is known

for highly pedestrianized streets and neighborhoods as well as expansive and well-defined public open spaces. It is generally considered a green and highly livable city with a comprehensive public transportation system. Tourism, cultural venues and central locations for international organizations have all prospered in Paris. The city's neighborhoods and political electorate are organized around 20 arrondissements, each directly electing a council which in turn elects an arrondissement mayor. A selection of members from each arrondissement council then forms the Council of Paris which elects the Mayor of Paris.

While it is not possible to generalize a standard European city model when considering the wide diversity of cultural traditions on the continent, it is informative to characterize recognizable features as we consider Paris. The normative European city is generally a dense and compact urban community assembled around an historic core. This has often had the effect of preserving the integrity of its traditional building fabric and open spaces. High density and physical compaction have favored both pedestrian-friendly environments as well as a range of tenancies within neighborhoods, creating a complex mixed-use environment combining residences, work, retail and leisure. While in Paris, this led over time to a high degree of social integration in the inner city with a general reduction in ghetto formation based upon income, origin or race, more recent problems of affordable housing and large working and non-working immigrant populations underserved at the city's perimeter remain significant challenges.

As an urban Industrial Revolution emerged in the nineteenth century, factories, residences, and ultimately automobiles, co-mingled, creating significant health and quality of life issues. In the twentieth century, economic activity continued to grow and become more specialized as city officials and modern architects worked to rezone Paris, redirecting industry and certain residential uses to the suburbs. As a result, the character of the central city was largely preserved while a combination of private vehicles and an expanding public transportation system served the outlying and growing neighborhoods.

Notwithstanding the aforementioned zoning and migrations, the singular historic event which defines Paris today is the work of Baron Haussmann, under the direction of Napoleon III. Carving grand boulevards through medieval neighborhoods as a method of both social engineering (moving military troops through the city) and beautification (giving privilege of place and amenities to the public right of way), Paris street patterns retain their medieval quirkiness as well their Cartesian overlay of boulevards and axially-located plazas and monuments. While these grand open spaces provided apt settings for the emerging and increasingly fashionable bourgeoisie, they also initiated a trend of pushing the less affluent populations to the perimeter under much less hospitable circumstances. Mid-twentieth century inner city slum clearance projects added to this trend. The site of the Pompidou Center was originally razed in 1939 as part of such a project. During the next round of similar clearance efforts in the 1960s and 70s, the great iron and glass food halls at Les Halles were torn down along with many of the bars and cafes in the area, considered at that time to be congested and antiquated.

By the 1970s and timed to align with the development of other Western cities that had become automobile dependent, hundreds of miles of freeway planning were well underway with a proposal for one along the Seine as well as one which would further expand the Peripherique. In the process, many older neighborhoods were again demolished and generic apartment blocks and public housing projects replaced them. The singular event, however, which crystallized Paris' desire to banish tall buildings from the historic city, and finally exorcized Le Corbusier's phantom visions to demolish and rebuild Europe's most beautiful city, was the construction, in 1972, of La Tour Maine-Montparnasse, a tower erected near the Luxembourg Gardens. Following an immediate national uproar, all high-rises were soon thereafter banned from the city center.

For some time, however, civic and business leaders in France had been aware of a growing corporate culture and the need to accommodate an increase in large-scale office space. Within the decade following World War II, economic growth was steady and upward and in 1958, the French government identified the La Defense district as a new hub for economic development and high-rise buildings. Following the debacle of La Tour, all new tall buildings were located at the Peripherique and beyond, most notably in La Defense.

PG_138_PERFORMATIVE_SKYSCRAPER_CHAPTER-FIVE.

Paris Skyline

In order to execute and oversee the new La Defense district, L'Establissement Public pour l'Amenagement de la Defense (EPAD) was established. Since its inception, EPAD has overseen the development of over 30 million square feet of office space for some 1500 corporate tenants. As the center of Paris' regional economy, over 150,000 commuters arrive at La Defense daily, by auto and rail. The district is 15 minutes by Metro from central Paris.

The master plan of La Defense centers on a wide slab of open space which runs one-half mile long in an attempt to visually connect von Spreckelsen's Grande Arche, the area's signature architectural element, along an axis through the Arc de Triomphe to the Louvre. It would be hard to imagine two more different paradigms of city planning than the historic city of Paris at one end and the scrum of modern commercial towers, familiar to major cities worldwide, at the other.

EPAD controls all physical development that relates to public spaces above and below the ground. One third of the plan area has been dedicated to pedestrian-only open space and the agency's planners have struggled to encourage additional and diverse uses to avoid the creation of a mono-functional eight-hour-a-day business community. With regard to architecture, individual property investors have a relatively free hand as they do with site programming and commercial development as long as they follow the building height constraints. Predictably, beyond the Arche and wide axial open space, La Defense looks like so many new Western business centers with variously configured super-blocks, individualized office towers and aimless ground planes.

After he took office in 2006, former President Nicolas Sarkozy convened a meeting of prominent architects to investigate the future of the city. His concerns were many: how to improve the city's working-class suburbs and how to build a greener Paris, the first city to meet the environmental goals of the Kyoto Accord. He wished to continue to preserve the historic city center while enhancing regional circulation and to plan for continuing de-industrialization and the global creative economy that is replacing it. Individual presentations were made from architects such as Richard Rogers, Jean Nouvel, Christian de Portzamparc and Bernardo Secchi which tended to be highly conceptual with long-term goals. Sarkozy asked the participants to collaborate and produce a more cohesive document but he was ousted by Francois Holland in 2011 and the visionary plans remain part of the archival and ongoing conversation about the nature of Paris' future.

In 2007, Sarkozy launched a comprehensive urban renewal project entitled the Grand Paris, aimed at better integrating outlying communities with the center of the historic city. While the project included cultural, housing, environmental and transport elements, the central component was a new 120 mile network of rapid transit lines aimed at connecting communities and establishing land-use overlays which, in some cases, set building height limits at 15 to 16 stories for housing and 50 stories for commercial buildings in areas tied to public transit. Notwithstanding the challenges of state finances, these plans are currently moving ahead during the presidency of Francois Hollande and targeted for completion in 2030.

Tokyo

The current population of Greater Tokyo is 12.6 million, however, Tokyo is a central part of Japan's Kanto Region which contains approximately 35 million inhabitants, making it the largest and most densely populated urban region in the world. Tokyo has a surface area of approximately 840 square miles with a residential density of 14,500 residents per square mile. While the aggregate population is high, with the exception of specific neighborhoods characterized by high-rise condominium towers, the city in general does not have a significant high-density residential core. Less than 5% of the city's total surface is dedicated to parks and open space. Japan perceives itself as a highly homogenous and cohesive island-nation. Currently less than half a million registered foreign residents, most from other East Asian countries, live in Tokyo, the country's capital and one of the world's acknowledged centers of economic activity, trading and financial services.

Tokyo is the largest metropolitan economy in the world with 51 of the Global 500 companies located in the city, contributing 18 per cent of the Japanese economy. While the city's business and service sectors employ 65 per cent of the labor force, Tokyo's manufacturing base, unlike those in other cities, remains steady at 15 per cent. Tokyo has a highly developed public transportation system; four out of five daily journeys in the city are by rail. The Greater Tokyo Government is divided into a central region of 23 wards with the western Tama area comprising the remaining megalopolis of 26 cities, 3 towns and one village. The importance of Tokyo to the State of Japan is underscored by the fact that the city receives more national fiscal resources than it contributes.

Since their contact with colonial powers in the 19th century, Japanese policy makers have been aware of the challenges of national survival in a world of increasing global trade. As a part of this national struggle, the capital city has been viewed by the Japanese as a symbol of Japan's industrial strength with a preponderance of national institutions and corporate headquarters located in the Greater Tokyo area. The growth this view has engendered in the city has been the source of ongoing conflict between corporate development and residents of central Tokyo. Political regimes and policies have changed over the years since World War II, but discontent persists. Current acrimony centers around real estate deregulation stemming from a desire to maintain a competitive global position in relation to the growing trade capitals of Shanghai, Hong Kong and Singapore. This ongoing effort to maintain its global business position has caused Japan to support research over the past three decades on the activities of "world cities" and those capital cities in the Asia Pacific region which encourage global trade and business formation.

Tokyo has had two great opportunities during the 20th century to lay groundwork for comprehensive urban master planning, the periods following the Great Kanto Earthquake of 1923 and World War II. These opportunities, however, were not exploited and the enormous growth that followed, particularly after the war, overtook the urge to adequately plan the city and insure an efficient and comprehensive infrastructure. During the rapid economic growth of the 1950s and 60s Japan had an extremely weak system of urban land planning and development control. An "iron triangle" coalition of the Liberal Democratic Party (LDP), the central government bureaucracy and big business cooperated to mobilize available natural resources and produce spectacular economic growth.

Following the war, Japan's focus was on industrial development and capital formation in an attempt to rebuild the state and assume a competitive position in world markets. Accordingly, revenues were constantly redirected to growth and reinvestment and little was made available for social programs and infrastructure. The housing supply was left to the private sector and only during emergencies and natural disasters was public action taken. Urban policy was narrowly focused on prioritizing economic development and the role of city planning was intended only to provide minimal infrastructure in order to facilitate growth. The main planning tool was a weak zoning system comprised of 4 zones: residential, commercial, industrial and quasi-industrial. Within each zoning area, land development was granted as-of-right, with no requirements for real estate developers to provide any public infrastructure along with private project development, no subdivision control, nor any minimum housing equivalence. The result was extremely rapid growth of under-serviced commercial sprawl at high densities.

This weak planning system was very much the product of strong central control wherein local governments have been highly dependent on financial grants from the central government. Because, planning legislation in this period was typically written and interpreted by central government ministries, planning tools available to local governments were severely limited. While in the immediate aftermath of the war, there was broad agreement within Japan that reconstruction and economic growth were top priorities, by the 1960's that consensus began to break down due to environmental problems growing out of unrestricted development. Large-scale development of heavy and chemical industries close to residential and commercial areas fostered air, water and food pollution which led to environmental degradation and health care concerns.

As urban residents faced off against lax government and big business, the political left came to power. Much of the electorate became convinced that the conservative central government and its allies were responsible for pollution, the lack of social programs and the disproportionate support of business interests over those of residents. The New City Planning Law of 1968 became the first post-war document to foster hope that local governments might receive the tools they needed to control and improve the qualitative development of their urban environments.

Short-lived, the new planning system failed to control development at the fringes of Tokyo but for a brief period created Exclusive Residential Zone #1, the first land use zone to meaningfully restrict land uses, heights and densities. The new system mandated an absolute height limit of 10 meters within the newly-defined zone. The tradition of low height limits was considered to be important in the building code due to the legacy of earthquakes and the importance of access to sunlight in Japanese homes. In the 1970s, however, owing to improvements in engineering technology and the widespread use of steel-reinforced concrete, revisions were made to the Building Standards Law abolishing building height limits. Residents continued to battle taller and high-density development throughout the 1970s and by the end of the decade, some limitation on the unregulated construction of high-rise buildings had been achieved.

By the early 1980s, urban policies once again experienced a shift. The new Prime Minister, Yasuhiro Nakasone, influenced by the neoliberal policies of Thatcher and Reagan, promoted deregulation, privatization and fiscal retrenchment. This was pursued in the interest of international competitiveness while city planning tools used to limit and control real estate development disappeared throughout the decade. Notable among the growing support for greater height and density in Tokyo was a new and widely-used planning measure modeled on New York City's Plaza Bonus system of two decades earlier which rewarded developers with extra height and floor area allowances in return for

Tokyo Skyline

providing public open space at the ground level. This trend toward plazas at the bases of tall buildings allowed the features of Modern architecture and Western-style corporate culture to come to Tokyo, playing to the public's desire for more publicly accessible open space in a crowded city.

Parallel to efforts to densify the inner city were plans to support a vision of polycentric development within the greater Tokyo area. Building upon the sense of a historic city center with radial transportation spokes out to the adjoining communities, this vision identified specific centers for dense urban development along these spokes and described a periphery of arterials, greenbelt and harbor. Reminiscent and synchronous with visions for polycentric Los Angeles, London and Paris, one of the most visionary subcenters was conceived to be built on reclaimed land in Tokyo Bay.

As a new satellite center, Tokyo Teleport Town was planned to function as Japan's central international communications gateway with high quality office space suited to the clustering of high technology enterprises. As the Japanese economy boomed throughout the 1980s, central Tokyo continued to develop apace. At the end of the decade, the economic bubble burst and the Tokyo Bay vision plan was abandoned.

More recently, the ongoing recession has again tipped the political advantage in favor of the property development industry, this time with new urgencies, one domestic, the other global. On the domestic front, for over two decades, Japan has been attempting to restore its financial system after near collapse due to massive real estate loan defaults, a crash in equity values and the devaluation in land prices since 1991. As a result, the government has been providing financial bailouts to banks as well as initiating spending on infrastructure in support of the construction and real estate development industries. On the global front, shifts in trade alliances are making other East Asian cities such as Singapore, Shanghai and Hong Kong viable regional competitors. Once again, business interests are making a case to the central government that commercial real estate must remain globally competitive. As a result, in 2002, the Koizumi government passed the Special Urban Regeneration Act (SURA) and established an Urban Regeneration Office within the national cabinet. This office has direct control over the granting of density bonuses and the regulation of height limits, bypassing local governments and community opposition. In addition to these policies, the Tokyo Metropolitan Government has, over time, announced The Tokyo Plan 2000, the 2001 New City Planning Vision for Tokyo and the Housing Master Plan for Tokyo 2001-2015, all highly coordinated with SURA.

Like so many world cities, the central government is attempting to create an environment hospitable to the international business community within its capital. In this context, global power is often defined as a mixture of premium high-rise office space, the centrality of financial and commodities markets and the synergies of high-end retail, residence and hospitality. While Japan is a liberal democratic state with enormous economic clout, decision-making authority over urban development has waffled between central and local control. As markets continue to become more global and the competition with its regional neighbors intensifies, the policy pendulum swings back to the central government in pursuing economic power, higher densities and tall buildings in Tokyo.

Shanghai

Greater Shanghai is a city-state. Spread over 2400 square miles, it has more than 18 million inhabitants. City boundaries define an area of 112 square miles in which 6.5 million people live at densities up to ten times the average density of London; parts of Shanghai's Huangpo district contain as many as 320,000 people per square mile. Most of Shanghai's territory is considered urbanized and reaches an average density of 7,500 residents per square mile. While the central core is continuing to densify, sprawl is moving out of core areas and into satellite cities and medium-sized towns. Given its low fertility rates, the demographic growth in Shanghai is now driven by immigration, the massive relocation of rural Chinese to the city as well as foreign immigrants, both groups generally providing the low-wage labor required to serve the rapid economic development of the city. Additionally, much of the population is graying; 17 per cent of Shanghai residents are 65 years or older.

Since the 1980s, the Shanghai economy has grown by as much as 15 per cent per year and is expected to continue well into the next decade, if at slightly lower rates. Approximately half of the labor force now works in the service sector while Shanghai's wider economic base, the Yangtze River Delta, makes up 22 per cent of China's Gross Domestic Product. Shanghai continues to invest heavily in its road capacity and public transportation systems in order to mobilize this region.

The Shanghai Municipal government is divided into 19 districts, however, these local administrations have limited planning power and frequently compete for investment. The Mayor of Shanghai is extremely powerful as he oversees the economic development of the city and region and is very tied to the central government which exercises control over investment and growth. Both Jiang Zemin and Zhu Rongji, former heads of state, had been mayors of Shanghai.

China is undergoing an extraordinary urban revolution of unprecedented scale. While the population is historically rooted in an agricultural economy and village culture, the swift and modernizing events of the past three decades suggests that by 2015, more than half the population of China will live in urban areas. The projected urban population of 700 million is larger than that of any country except India. Today, Shanghai is poised to become China's premiere global city competing directly with Hong Kong, Tokyo and Singapore.

Shanghai has experienced three distinct cultural evolutions in the modern period. From 1840 until 1949, colonial capitalism reigned with Shanghai functioning as a major trading port. Accessed by way of the many tributaries of the great Yangtze River leading into China, parallel European trading colonies co-existed within Shanghai.

No settlement existed on the Pudong side of the Huang Po River, however, the Bund was intensively developed by the standards of the day and took shape as a fully-formed European colonial city.

During the Mao Zedong years and the founding of socialist China (1949-1980), the city's activities were overseen by a series of hybrid administrations. Within the socialist political context, Shanghai was seen by central ideological planning as a "producer city." As such, the city became the target location for state-owned industries and grew into a regional engine for economic growth under rigid central planning. The state prevented the city from generating population growth and building the commercial and municipal infrastructures that normally accompany rapid industrialization. Rural populations were kept out of the city just as collective worker compounds were kept in. In the socialist city, there existed no labor market and the workplace was state-owned and heavily politicized. During this period, the state established a policy of distributing economic and technical resources to needier interior cities and, as a "producer city," physical improvements in Shanghai stagnated while the city continued to export more goods and economic capital than it received from the central government.

In the 1980s and in the wake of Mao's passing, the central government turned away from comprehensive state socialism and selected four initial experimental cities (Shenzen, Zhuhai, Shantou, and Xiamen) and, subsequently, fourteen larger cities along the coastal belt. Shanghai was among the latter group, proposed to be "open cities." These cities received financial incentives and flexibility in dealing with foreign investors and they were allowed to experiment with market reforms rather than centralized policy. The boom in commercial and industrial development came when the state allowed a number of these cities to also exercise the right to lease state-owned land to foreign investors in the mid to late 1980s. With land costs effectively at zero, significant net revenues began coming in by leasing that valuable land for factories, corporate headquarters and office buildings. Cities such as Shanghai generated enormous revenues, enabling them to build out the infrastructure which would support further boom development. The ongoing economic success of capitalizing this state land to encourage further foreign investment appeared to justify the policy of state-led urban development.

Now, with receding centralized socialist policies, the labor market is evolving and becoming more highly differentiated. In Chinese cities and towns, for example, the share of employment in the state sector has dropped from 70 per cent in 1992 to 25 per cent in 2004. Cultural changes are now underway, however, as many job applicants with high-level university degrees discover that college-level applicants with practical work experience are currently in greater demand. The relative sophistication of China's industrial markets is still in transition. Also, as multi-national corporations relocate to China and factories proliferate, Chinese employees are familiarized with international brands and local consumption patterns change, favoring brand names and luxury items.

In Shanghai, the high-rise building has enjoyed a history of over 90 years. The first era was the Neoclassical and Art Deco high-rise period of the 1920s and 30s when European traders colonized the city, then came the first period of economic reform and liberalization of the 1980s. In central Shanghai, this new wave of tall buildings was designed by institutional American architects such as John Portman and Ellerbe Becket, large firms which had developed and innovated the post-World War II commercial building type. As the type proliferated in an environment with no tall building legacy and little competition, the urban landscape became defined by numerous, bland residential and office towers of medium height.

During this time, China underwent much soul-searching with regard to what constituted appropriate Chinese architecture for its growing collection of tall buildings, increasing with particular speed in cities like Shanghai. Research into Hong Kong's more modern legacy with its carefully managed state land bank and auctions provided cues. As a generation of new buildings began to take hold, Shanghai staged an international architectural competition for a redevelopment master plan for the Pudong area. Many celebrated architects participated including Toyo Ito, Massimiliano Fuksas and Richard Rogers among them. Each put forward radical concepts for planning the district. Then, in a process familiar to western architects working in China, the city government claimed to take the best features from each of them, began to auction large land

Shanghai Skyline

parcels and moved forward with development at characteristically break-neck speed. Like so many master plan efforts of that period, the final outcomes bore no resemblance to the competition presentations but, rather, provided a road map for commercial land parcelization.

In 1990, China's central government announced to the world a plan to open Pudong for development. The authorities considered this to be an opportunity to create an international business, finance and trade center as well as to serve as a regional stimulus to the Yangtze River Delta and the entire Yangtze River Valley. The head of state at the time and the architect of China's reform, Deng Xiaoping, initiated and promoted the undertaking personally. President Jiang Zemin reinforced the importance to China of developing special economic zones such as the Pudong New District.

These zones would lead the country in innovation, industry and economic liberalization and provide models for regeneration throughout the State. In 1991, Pudong New District became a national project and received special economic zone status. One of the five sub-districts in particular, Lujiazui Finance and Trade Center epitomizes the policy and symbolizes Shanghai's high-rise architectural future, an area totaling 11 square miles.

Over 4000 high-rise buildings stood completed in Shanghai as of 2001 and hundreds have been added since. The total floor area is thought to be over one billion square feet, a figure far exceeding that of Hong Kong and certainly ranking it as the largest globally. The rapid pace of high-rise development has caused the Shanghai Municipality to exert some measure of control on density and construction. In an attempt to achieve what it calls "surface low density," the Municipality has levied restrictions on floor area ratios, ratios which are frequently subverted through air rights transfers and the purchase of additional land area. Research into the environmental challenges of highly dense and tall cities has led to the Chinese government using the 2008 Beijing Olympics followed by the World Expo 2010 in Shanghai as experimental sites for exploring the greening, amenitization and quality of life available to inner city dwellers.

Assuming that anything like the current economic and physical growth in China continues, the main challenge for a city like Shanghai is how it will succeed in balancing the needs of its expanding population with a healthy and high standard of living. As it stands, Shanghai has fixed its current population inside the central ring road at 15 million. There are approximately 60 million residents undergoing some level of urbanization in the area around Shanghai, a broad, flat plain without natural boundaries.

The Municipality has identified 11 satellite towns targeted for the region outside the ring road. As these towns are designed, built and occupied (each is planned for a population of between 500,000 and 1 million), they will require a constantly growing network of improved highways, rail lines and open space. With the center virtually built out, the options for density going forward are few. One choice appears to be building tall high-density satellite cities around the periphery of Shanghai so that the region is populated with similar urban centers with substantial open space and natural systems between. Another would be to build out a more uniform carpet of low-rise medium density development, promising a homogeneity which might blur the distinction between nature and the urban environment. In either case, significant infrastructure will be required and social and spatial equality will need to improve as growth continues at this extraordinary pace.

Abu Dhabi

The city of Abu Dhabi is the capital of the Emirate of Abu Dhabi and the federal capital of the United Arab Emirates (U.A.E.), a sovereign country of seven emirates on the Arabian Gulf. The city is the largest municipality in the Emirate of Abu Dhabi, which, at 26,000 square miles, is the largest of the emirates, covering 87 per cent of the country. The city is both the country's center for political and industrial activities as well as the major cultural and commercial center for the Emirate. Abu Dhabi alone generates approximately sixty per cent of the Gross Domestic Product of the U.A.E and is the wealthiest of the emirates in terms of per capita income. With a population of just over 600,000, GDP per capita is approximately $50,000 and the city holds investments in excess of $1 trillion worldwide. About a quarter of the population is made up of UAE nationals alongside large expatriate communities from India, Pakistan, Africa, Sri Lanka and the Philippines.

The city of Abu Dhabi is shaped like an elongated triangle and is situated on Abu Dhabi Island on the Gulf coastline extending to the mainland and neighboring islands. Residential settlements date to 1761. Until the mid-twentieth century, culture in the region centered around Bedouin practices of seasonal ranching and pearl-diving. Little merchant tradition existed in this clan-based society where the Nahyan family governed and provided continuous state oversight and intervention.

Change came in 1953 when the British negotiated offshore oil leases with the family and royalty payments began. With the first exports of oil in 1962, the municipality was established and its first public improvements consisted of measures to improve the standard of living with the provision of food, health services and adequate drinking water. While conservative and slow to act, the municipality eventually began to create gridded road systems and public works programs for government buildings, airport, desalination and electricity plants, green open spaces and the dredging of canals around the island. Finally, many residents were relocated from traditional Bedouin residences and housed in new and more modern homes.

In 1968, Abdel Rahman Makhlouf, an Egyptian planner who had initiated town planning efforts in Jeddah, Saudi Arabia, arrived and became the Director General of Town Planning for Abu Dhabi. During his term, he attempted to create a "national house," adapting Bedouin culture to an urban domestic lifestyle. He worked to modernize the souq, or market, and he set maximum building height standards at 8 to 10 stories. Throughout the 70s, height limits were revised up to 13 stories with a few exceptions such as 20 stories for the two luxury hotels of the day.

In the 1980s and 90s, the Khalifa Committee (named after Sheik Zayed's son and the current ruler of Abu Dhabi and the UAE) was in operation, distributing state-owned land to Emirati citizens and overseeing the construction of countless apartment blocks. During this period, over 200 apartment buildings were constructed each year in the central city on small plots not larger than 30 meters square and averaging 20 stories in height. These buildings were generally highly repetitive and uninspired due to the fact that the Committee oversaw a highly centralized process wherein it would control design, construction and the revenue aspects of development. During this period, Abu Dhabi nationals received housing, land and a major income stream while the Sheik and municipality kept land out of the hands of foreign residents and investors. The rapid modernization effort of this period has resulted in a city center characterized today by the contrast between aging mid-rise towers from the 70's and 80's and more recent and taller ultra-modern towers.

Comparisons to its sister-emirate, Dubai, a two hour drive away, are unavoidable, particularly as they relate to real estate investment and tall buildings. Symbolizing this comparison, the former Burj Dubai, the world's tallest building, was re-named Burj Kalifa, following an infusion from Abu Dhabi of 10 billion dollars on behalf of the project during recessionary times. Historically, the Nahyan family of Abu Dhabi represented conservative Bedouin values and was slow to begin to modernize the city, whereas the Maktoum family of Dubai had a merchant background and developed a more speculative and aggressive vision for propelling Dubai into a commercial future.

Whereas Abu Dhabi lacks meaningful historic structures, is conservative and does not display the liberal entertainment venues of its rival, Dubai has an established historic core, is cosmopolitan, more liberal and is attempting to make itself available as a central trading hub between Eastern and Western countries. Abu Dhabi has, at least until recently, looked to be a center of regional, Islamic power. Whereas Dubai has encouraged foreign investment in its extraordinary building program and created venues for foreign ownership in real estate, igniting a highly speculative building market, Abu Dhabi has only recently opened foreign real estate investment to long-term lease participation in its building market. To understand the true co-dependence of the two capital cities, it should be understood that Dubai's boom relied upon the wealth of its neighbor just as Dubai benefited from the restricted investment opportunities within Abu Dhabi itself. Abu Dhabi, for its part, is now using Dubai as a belated model for much of its own real estate development policy, opening up to foreign investment and relaxing its participation restrictions.

The year 2004 witnessed the death of Sheikh Zayed and the transfer of power to Kalifa. Among a range of modernizing trends, one of the most important was the change in property ownership law which allowed, for the first time, the sale of government-granted land by nationals as well as the introduction of a form of ownership by foreigners through the purchase of 99 year leaseholds in specially designated investment zones. The centralized welfare state has begun to shift to one which accommodates corporate and private investment activity. The city had kept a low-profile until 2004 even as it amassed significant oil and gas revenues, investing internationally through its main overseas financial arm, the Abu Dhabi Investment Authority (ADIA). With the evolution of the city, its political stability and this important change in property law, significant Arab capital is now repatriating to Abu Dhabi, finding investment opportunities again in real estate.

In 2007, as the economy continued to expand and real estate speculation followed, the Abu Dhabi Urban Planning Council (UPC) was created to oversee development in the city and the emirate as a whole. Focused on four elements of sustainability: the natural environment, social development, economic development and cultural heritage, the UPC has produced the Plan Abu Dhabi 2030: Urban Structure Framework Plan. Projecting a population growth to 3 million by 2030, the policies contained therein focus on Arab identity and sustainability. The plan states that Abu Dhabi will be a "contemporary expression of an Arab city" and will continue to practice measured growth, will respect the natural environment of coastal and desert ecologies and will physically express its role as the capital city of the UAE.

Various strategies in the Plan will be employed to mediate the natural environment with a "green gradient" of parks and open spaces connecting the coastline to the desert through

PG_150_PERFORMATIVE_SKYSCRAPER_CHAPTER-FIVE.

Abu Dhabi Skyline

the urban neighborhoods. Sand belts and "desert fingers" are imagined to limit the extent of urbanization into nature. In terms of density and land use, two areas of concentrated growth are targeted, one being the new CBD adjacent to the historic city, the other being the Capital City District on the mainland of Abu Dhabi adjacent to the Abu Dhabi International Airport. While both are planned to be major mixed-use centers, the CBD is targeted for business, retail and commercial office uses. CCD will be oriented to medical centers, higher education and government buildings.

Behind the strategy to foster two urban centers in Abu Dhabi is the desire to limit ultimate density in the historic CBD, already limited as it is by its island geometry, and to create an expansion satellite that can absorb greater growth. The concept of two polar mixed-use centers also reinforces a simplified transportation system connecting the two with public transit rail, high-speed rail and freight rail plus a surface network of buses, streetcars and a fine-grained system of city streets for local circulation. The mixed-use zoning is an attempt to pedestrianize local traffic whenever possible. Building height and the regulation of tall buildings is organized around the idea of protecting view corridors to the Grand Mosque, planned government buildings and monuments.

Finally, in its attempt to diversify its economy away from gas and oil, Abu Dhabi has initiated a range of programs to bolster cultural tourism by connecting itself to the global centers of art and culture. The planning and development of Saadiyat Island, located approximately 1500 feet from the main shoreline of Abu Dhabi and encompassing an area of 10 square miles, goes back to the early 1990s when it was initially planned as a financial center. More recent master planning efforts target it for a major cultural destination including a satellite Guggenheim Museum, a classical museum affiliated with the Louvre, a maritime museum, performing arts center and nineteen assorted fine arts pavilions all designed by a variety of international architects.

São Paulo

With nearly 11 million residents, São Paulo is the largest city in Brazil and the world's seventh largest city by population. Compared to the United States' Combined Statistical Area (CSA), the São Paulo megalopolis is the world's third largest at 27 million inhabitants, behind only Tokyo and Jakarta. Owing to its history of immigration, the population is both ethnically diverse and interracial. São Paulo is the capital of the state of São Paulo and generates the largest Gross Domestic Product among all Latin American cities. At $14,000, its GDP per capita is the second highest among Latin American cities, behind only Brasilia.

São Paulo is considered the financial capital of Brazil and is the location for headquarters of many major corporations, banks and financial institutions. Its GDP makes up over 12 per cent of Brazil's national total and it produces 36 per cent of all goods and services in the State of São Paulo, the most populous Brazilian state. Once known for its strong industrial sector, the city's economy has become increasingly based upon service and business.

The city is divided into 31 prefectures which are each divided into 96 districts. Locally, districts may contain one or more neighborhoods. The prefectures are grouped into nine regions taking into account their geography and history. These regions are organized for government administrative purposes and have no natural physical boundaries nor do they display any outward identification.

São Paulo officially became a city in 1711. In the 19th century, it experienced economic prosperity through coffee exports shipped from neighboring areas. In the early years of the 20th century, the price of coffee had plummeted owing to international trade pressure and, subsequently, the Wall Street Crash of 1929. Looking for other economic alternatives, business interests had by then turned to the production and export of sugar cane and alcohol. During this period of growth and following the abolition of slavery in 1888, waves of immigration ensued, both from European countries as well as inter-regionally, as populations pursued work and prosperity. São Paulo maintained a high economic growth rate throughout the 1920s by way of rapid industrialization and investment. During this period, the Sampaio Moreira Building reached an unprecedented 14 stories in height and by the end of the decade; the Martinelli Building was topped off at twice that height.

Between 1920 and 1940, the city's population more than doubled to 1.3 million and although modernity had begun to emerge in the better neighborhoods of São Paulo by the 1930s, vast areas remained poor and unchanged. No city plan existed before 1889 and no zoning legislation occurred until 1972. By 1950, the city added another one million residents and the tallest building was the São Paulo State Bank building, soon to be overtaken by Oscar Niemeyer's architecturally memorable Copan Building and the Italia Building. By the 1960s São Paulo included nearly half the population of the State of São Paulo and accounted for one-third of the country's total employment. The concentration of such density resulted in a wide range of highway expansion projects and mass transit programs, many underway for decades but failing to keep up with widening suburban sprawl. The underground subway system, begun in 1968, extends only 36 miles and there are only 16 miles of bicycle lanes, 12 of which are in public parks. Over a thousand private helicopters are registered in the city, allegedly making up the largest fleet in the world. Additionally, as the historic center of the city has deteriorated since the 1970s, newer buildings have been sited in peripheral suburbs, causing the center to fall further into disrepair and abandon. Eighteen per cent of the center's buildings are vacant, many of which have been empty for more than a decade. A significant dislocation has developed over the years between job opportunities and residential neighborhoods spread over great distances within the city. This has led to disproportionately long distances traveled by many employees, taxing the already strained transportation system.

The periphery of São Paulo continues to expand.

Approximately 35 per cent of the city is environmentally protected in theory, much of it occupied by the Guarapiranga and Billings dams which provide water to city residents. Realistically, however, the protected lands are increasingly encroached by favelas, informal settlements of wooden shacks. More than 1.6 million people are currently living in the catchment areas of the two dams. Informal and illegal connections to both water and sewer systems compromise the water quality and service for the rest of the city. These highly dense and vulnerable ad hoc communities are concentrated in areas most poorly served by social, recreational and employment opportunities.

While São Paulo evolved from a village to a city over time, the metropolis that is recognizable today was formed in the 20th century. Through a series of actions, protests and projects, the process of urban planning has been episodic and informal rather than centrally planned. Typically, plans were introduced throughout the century which took their cues from the informal logic of the city's existing street plan. However, in the mid-1950s, plans submitted by former Mayor Prestes Maia São Paulo (known as the Avenues Plan) took a Haussmannian approach of creating strong axial roadways through a "demolish and rebuild" approach to the city fabric.

In 1968, the Basic Plan for Integrated Development of São Paulo was announced during the administration of Figueiredo Ferraz, introducing zoning laws adopted in 1972. The principal feature of the law was a simplified zoning system in which elite residential zones were identified and protected under a Zone 1 designation while Zone 2 designation referred to the remainder of the city and was non specific in its requirements and limitations. This resulted in conditions whereby wealthy homes were protected while the remainder of São Paulo was loosely defined, allowing evacuation of the historic core and the densification and development of prosperous new business centers in the peripheral suburbs. It has been in these areas where both the intersection of corporate relocation, lax regulation and real estate speculation has led to some of São Paulo's tallest new buildings.

The historic core of the city has been in significant decline for fifty years. It contains, among other important landmarks, São Paulo's legacy of historic tall buildings.

Like many other 20th century cities, the middle-class had begun to evacuate the city center decades ago. As this trend gained force, vast expressways, interchanges, widened rights-of-way and parking lots increased in number. Commercial and residential buildings were left standing as islands in a widening sea of asphalt and moving automobile traffic. This trend and a decided lack of public transportation discouraged pedestrianization and bicycle traffic, first causing the ground plane to become economically non-viable and ultimately, accelerating the exodus of more affluent residents and high-value economic tenants. The desirability of the city center plummeted and became available largely to the influx of poor rural immigrants seeking employment and those without any other practical choice.

In an attempt to reverse these trends, Vivo o Centro, created in 1991 and funded by large downtown-based banks, launched the first official comprehensive rehabilitation effort in the city center. Since then, The Institute for Transportation and Development Policy (ITDP) has created walkable plans within the city center through a mix of street pedestrianization, bicycle plan expansion, and auto congestion pricing policies. Attempts to create Business Improvement Districts (BID) are underway to insure safety and maintenance of the public right-of-way while historic buildings are slowly beginning to be renovated. The Central Market has been restored and two historic railroad stations have been converted into cultural institutions. While the ultimate outcome is still uncertain, there is hope that these plans can begin to entice the creative class back to the city center with cultural and entertainment venues, higher education opportunities, research, development and design. Should these efforts prevail, it now seems possible to imagine a re-inhabitation and restoration of the many historic tall buildings in the heart of São Paolo even as new towers continue to be designed and built throughout the city.

[21] Clark, Greg, *London and New York in the 21st Century. New Competition and New Opportunities: Can London and New York Still Be the Leading World Cities in 2100,* op. cit.

PG_154_PERFORMATIVE_SKYSCRAPER_CHAPTER-FIVE.

PG_155_PERFORMATIVE_CITIES.

São Paulo Skyline

BIBLIOGRAPHY

"Abu Dhabi." *Wikipedia.com.* Wikipedia.com, n.d. Web. 25 Nov. 2012.

"Abu Dhabi's Sun Sensitive Twin Towers." *Phaidon.com.* Phaidon.com, n.d. Web. 27 Sept. 2012.

"AD Classics: National Library of France / Dominique Perrault." *Archdaily.com.* Archdaily.com, n.d. Web. 17 Sept. 2012.

Aiello, Carlo. "eVolo: 2010 Skyscraper Competition." *eVolo* Fall 2010: 25-38. Print.

Allen, Jim. "Sustainable Retrofits : The Future of Green Building." *Pmengineer.com.* N.p., 1 May 2008. Web. 18 June 2012.

Alter, Lloyd. "Design / Sustainable Design." *Treehugger.com.* Treehugger.com, 13 July 2011. Web.

Annereau, Nigel, Damian Eley, and James Thonger. "The Leadenhall Building." *The Arup Journal 2* (2013): 67-76. Print.

Arak, Joey. "Jean Nouvel's MoMA Tower Reimagined As... This!" *Ny.curbed.com.* Ny.curbed.com, 16 July 2009. Web.

"Art Science Museum Singapore." *E-architect.co.uk.* E, 23 Feb. 2011. Web.

Ascher, Kate. The Heights: *Anatomy of a Skyscraper.* N.p.: Penguin HC, The, 2011. Print.

"Axis Mundi Unveils Conceptual Design for MoMA Tower." *Designboom.com.* Designboom.com, n.d. Web. 13 June 2012.

Bagli, Charles V. "Will A Tower Block the Empire State Building." *The New York Times* 24 Aug. 2010: A18. Print.

Bagli, Charles V. "Bloomberg Pushes a Plan to Let Midtown Soar." *The New York Times* 7 Oct. 2012: 1. Print.

Bagli, Charles V. "Sky High and Going Up Fast: Luxury Towers Take New York." *The New York Times* 19 May 2013: 1+. Print.

Bagli, Charles V. "Feature at Trade Center Is Halted After $10 Million." *Nytimes.com.* Nytimes.com, 11 May 2011. Web.

Bagli, Charles V. "With Partner Selected, Trade Center Project Discredits Some Naysayers." *The New York Times* 8 July 2010: A19. Print.

Banham, Reyner. "Architecture of the Well-Tempered Environment". Second Edition ed. N.p.: University Of Chicago, 1984. Print.

Barbanel, Josh. "Sky - High Loses Altitude." *The New York Times* 23 Nov. 2008, Real Estate sec.: 2. Print.

Barrionuevo, Alexei. "Another Tower for the Skyline." *The New York Times* 4 Oct. 2012, Real Estate sec.: 9. Print.

Barrionuevo, Alexei. "Staking a Claim in South America." *The New York Times* 24 Mar. 2013: 11. Print.

Basulto, David. "Sky Village In Rodovre / MVRDV." *Arch.* N.p., n.d. Web.

Basulto, David. "Sky Village In Rodovre / MVRDV." *Archdaily.com.* Archdaily.com, 10 Nov. 2008. Web.

"Behold the Bigness of Brazil." *The New York Times Magazine* 3 Mar. 2013: 30-37. Print.

Belesky, Philip. "Ghost in the Machines: Parametric Architecture and the Philosophy of Giles Deleuze." *Manifoldblog.com.* Manifoldblog.com, n.d. Web. 5 May 2013.

Bellafante, Gina. "Building High Anxiety." *The New York Times* 24 Mar. 2013: 22. Print.

Benyus, Janine M. *Biomimicry.* N.p.: William Morrow, 2002. Print.

Bierig, Aleksandr. "Envisioning Green." *The GreenSource* Nov.-Dec. 2009: 106-09. Print.

"BIG Architects: Cross # Towers, Seoul, Korea." *Designboom.com.* Designboom.com, n.d. Web. 28 Sept. 2012.

"BIG Contributes to Towering Design in Seoul." Worldarchitecturenews.com. *Worldarchitecturenews.com,* 03 May 2012. Web.

"A BIG New York Debut: West 57th." *Archdaily.com.* Archdaily.com, n.d. Web. 18 Sept. 2012.

Bogosian, Biayna. "Unfolding Azadi Tower: Reading Persian Folds Through Deleuze." *Thefunambulist.net.* Thefunambulist.net, 9 Aug. 2011. Web. 30 Aug. 2012.

Brake, Alan G., David D'Arcy, Julie V. Lovine, Danielle Rago, and Aaron Seward. "Las Vegas Is Learning." *The Architects Newspaper* 13 Aug. 2008: 17-21. Print.

Brownell, Blaine. *Material Strategies: Innovative Applications in Architecture.* N.p.: Princeton Architectural, 2011. Print.

Brownell, Blaine. "Two (More) Towers." *Architect Sept.* 2011: 116. Print.

Buchanan, Peter. "The Tower: An Anachronism Awaiting Rebirth." *Harvard Design Magazine* n.d.: 5+. Web.

Burdett, Ricky, and Deyan Sudjic. *The Endless City: The Urban Age Project by the London School of Economics and Deutsche Bank's Alfred Herrhausen Society.* N.p.: Phaidon, 2010. Print.

Burdett, Ricky, and Deyan Sudjic. *Living in the Endless City: The Urban Age Project by the London School of Economics and Deutsche Bank's Alfred Herrhausen Society.* N.p.: Phaidon, 2011. Print.

Bureau of Urban Development Tokyo Metropolitan Government. *Urban Development in Tokyo.* N.p.: n.p., 2011. Print.

"Caltrans District 7 Headquarters: Intensifies Circulation and Encourages Productive Social Exchange." *Morphomedia.com.* Morphomedia.com, 22 Feb. 2009. Web. 17 Sept. 2012.

Cassidy, Robert. "Ingenhoven Architects: Seeking Optimal Balance." *Bdcnetwork.com.* Bdcnetwork.com, 11 Aug. 2010. Web. 17 Sept. 2012.

Castells, Manuel. *The Informational City: Economic Restructuring and Urban Development.* N.p.: Wiley-Blackwell, 1992. Print

Chamberlain, Lisa. "MIT v. Holl: Controversy Heats up over One of the Most Celebrated Buildings in Recent Memory." *Metroplismag.com.* Metropolismag.com, 1 Nov. 2004. Web.

Chen, Aric. "KPF Crowns an Ever-Expanding Skyline with the Shanghai World Financial Center." *Architectural Record* May 2009: 164-90. Print.

Cities: Architecture and Society : 10th International Architecture Exhibition. Vol. 2. N.p.: Rizzoli, 2006. Print.

Cities: People, Society, Architecture : 10th International Architecture Exhibition. Vol. 1. N.p.: Rizzoli, 2006. Print.

"City Subtleties." *The Architectural Review* Oct. 2008: 60-61. Print.

Clark, Greg. *London and New York in the 21st Century. New Competition and New Opportunities: Can London and New York Still Be the Leading World Cities in 2100?* Rep. N.p., n.d. Web

Clark, Greg. "The Manhattanization of London?" *Urban Land* July 2008: 105-09. Print.

Clarke, Sean. "Foster's Gherkin Tipped for Architecture Prize." *Guardian.co.uk.* Guardian.co.uk, 9 Sept. 2004. Web. 13 July 2012.

"CLC Tower and MSFL Tower by REX." *Designitecture.com.* Designitecture.com, 25 Mar. 2012. Web. 9 Aug. 2012.

Cole, Russell, Mac Tan, and Alex Wong. "The Facades Systems." *The Arup Journal* (2012): 64-67. Print.

Collins, Alastair, Steve Watts, and Mark McAlister. "The Economics of Sustainable Tall Buildings." *The Big Project* Feb. 2008: n. pag. Print.

Cook, Julia. "Reforma Movement: Mexico's City's Iconic Avenue Is Experiencing an Incongruous Influx of Luxury High-rises." *Metropolis* Oct. 2008: 52. Print.

"The Cooper Union for the Advancement of Science and Art / Morphosis Architecture." *Archdaily.com.* Archdaily.com, n.d. Web. 17 Sept. 2012.

"COR Tower Miami." *E-architect.co.uk.* E-architect.co.uk, Mar. 2007. Web. 5 June 2012.

Davidson, Justin. "Colossus." *New York* 10 May 2010: 26-30. Print.

Davidson, Justin. "Higher: At the Skyscraper Museum, a Reminder of Why We Keep Reaching for the Clouds." *Nymag.com.* N.p., 14 Aug. 2011. Web. 19 Aug. 2011.

Davis, Mike. *Planet of Slums.* N.p.: Verso, 2007. Print.

Deleuze, Gilles, and Félix Guattari. *A Thousand Plateaus: Capitalism and Schizophrenia.* Minneapolis: University of Minnesota, 1987. Print.

"Deleuze and Space: The Smooth and the Striated." *Architectureandspace.com.* Architectureandspace.com, n.d. Web. 8 Sept. 2012.

Despommier, Dickson. "The Vertical Farm: An Alternate Method of Food Production Has Been Proposed-growing Large Amounts of Produce within the Confines of High-rise Building." *Urban Land* July 2008: 101-04. Web.

Despommier, Dickson. *The Vertical Farm: Feeding the World in the 21st Century.* New York: Picador, 2011. Print.

The Detailed View of the Nine WTC Site Proposals. Ny1.com, n.d. Web. 13 Sept. 2012.

Duffy, Frank. *Work and the City.* London: Black Dog, 2008. Print.

Dunlap, David W. "As Tower Rises, It's Not Quite What Was Planned." *The New York Times* 13 June 2012: A21. Print.

Dunlap, David W. "Up From Zero." *The New York Times* 5 Sept. 2010, Metropolitan sec.: 1. Print.

"Dynamic Hybrid: A Cluster of Towers Ingeniously Linked by a Vertiginous Bridge Inverts the Conventional Relationship between Tall Buildings and the Public Realm." *Architectural Review* Oct. 2008: 50-53. Print.

Elsheshtawy, Yasser. "Creating and Developing Islands in the United Arab Emirates." *Urban Land* Spring 2009: 45-51. Print.

Elsheshtawy, Yasser. *The Evolving Arab City: Tradition, Modernity and Urban Development.* Reprint Edition ed. N.p.: Routledge, 2011. Print.

Environmental Affairs Department City of Los Angeles. *Green Roofs - Cooling Los Angeles: A Resource Guide.* N.p.: n.p., n.d. Print.

"Federation of Korean Industries: AS + GG Design Head Office Building for Federation of Korean Industries in Seoul." *E-architect.co.uk.* E-architect.co.uk, 6 Jan. 2010. Web. 20 Sept. 2012.

"Federation of Korean Industries Tower: Adrian Smith + Gordon Gill Architecture's Seoul Tower Features a Pleated, BIPV - Paneled." *Archpaper.com.* Archpaper.com, 2 Nov. 2010. Web. 27 Sept. 2012.

Fessenden, Ford. "If You Where to Make a City." *The New York Times* 11 Sept. 2011: 18. Print.

Finn, Robin. "The Great Air Race." *The New York Times* 24 Feb. 2013, Real Estate sec.: 8. Print.

Flint, Graeme, David Healy, and Adam Monaghan. "Shard London Bridge." *The Arup Journal* 2 (2012): 93-97. Print.

Florida, Richard. "When The Sky Has It's Limits." *The Wall Street Journal* [New York] 4 Aug. 2012: W12. Print.

Fortmeyer, Russell. "Getting Aggressive About Passive Design." Continuingeducation.coonstruction.com. *Continuingeducation.coonstruction.com,* May 2007. Web. 14 June 2012.

Fortmeyer, Russell. "When Less Powers More." *Archrecord.construction.com.* Archrecord.construction.com, n.d. Web. 14 June 2012.

Fountain, Henry. "As Unbreakable as ...Glass?" *The New York Times* 7 July 2009: D1-D2. Print.

Fritz, Susanne. "Media Facade: A New Form of Art in Architecture." *Architonic.* Architonic, n.d. Web. 16 July 2012.

From Control to Design Parametric/Algorithmic Architecture. N.p.: Actar, 2008. Print.

Furuto, Alison. "Adrian Smith and Gordon Gill Architecture Win Competition for 4th Tallest Building in the World." *Archdaily.com.* Archdaily.com, 17 July 2011. Web. 17 Sept. 2012.

Furuto, Alison. "Beach and Howe Mixed-Used Tower / BIG." *Archdaily.com.* Archdaily.com, 17 Apr. 2012. Web.

Furuto, Alison. "First Certified "Green" Project in the Philippines." *Archdaily.com.* N.p., Feb. 2011. Web.

Furuto, Alison. "NYC Port Authority Bus Terminal: The World's Largest Media Facade." *Archdaily.com.* Archdaily.com, 14 June 2011. Web.

Gallagher, J.D., Ph.D., Mary C. "Skyscrapers Threaten the Horizon of Paris." *Blog.classicist.org.* Blog.classicist.org, 7 Aug. 2012. Web.

"Garden Tower : Wrapped in a Gridded Skin That Recalls a Traditional Masharabiya, This Tower in Riyadh Tempers and Tames Extremes of Climate." *The Architectural Review* Oct. 2008: 62-65. Print.

Gerber, David. *The Parametric Affect: Computation, Innovation and Models for Design Exploration in Contemporary Architectural Practice.* Cambridge, MA: The Harvard Graduate School of Design, 2009. Print.

Giedion, Sigfried, *Mechanization Takes Command.* 1st Edition ed. N.p.: Oxford Univ., 1948. Print

Gimbel, Barney. "The Richest City in the World: Ninety Miles from Dubai, Another Xanadu Has Been Decreed. Its Name Is Abu Dhabi, and That $3 Billion Hotel Is Just the Beginning of the Story." *Cnn.money.com.* Cnn.money.com, 12 Mar. 2007. Web. 6 Feb. 2008.

Goldberger, Paul. "The Skyline: Gracious Living." The New Yorker 7 Mar. 2011: 72. Print.

Goldberger, Paul. "Surface Tension: Jean Nouvel and the Art of the Facade." *Newyorker.com.* Newyorker.com, 23 Nov. 2009. Web. 17 Nov. 2009.

Gonchar, Joann. "8 House Bjarke Ingals Group." *Archrecord. construction.com.* Archrecord.construction.com, 8 Aug. 2011. Web.

Gonchar, Joann. "A Facade That Isn't Just Skin Deep." *Architectural Record* May 2012: n. pag. Print.

Gonchar, Joann. "Morphosis Architects: A Raw and Charismatic Vertical Campus Connects Students to Each Other and Their Urban Environment." *Archrecord.construction.com.* Archrecord.construction.com, n.d. Web. 17 Aug. 2012.

Gorsche, Jennifer K. "Growing Panes." *Architects Newspaper* 7 Dec. 2011: 10-11. Print.

Graham, Peter C. *The Parametric Facade.* Thesis. University of Waterloo, 2012. N.p.: n.p., n.d. Print.

Grayson, Nick. "CIS Tower Solar Skyscraper Retrofit." *Solarpedia.* Solarpedia, n.d. Web. 27 Aug. 2012.

"The Grey Lady: Renzo Piano Building Workshop Extends Its Reach in the United States, Designing Its First High Rise Tower, in Manhattan." *The Architectural Review* Apr. 2008: 42-52. Print.

"GSW Headquarters Berlin Germany." *Architecturerevived. blogspot.com.* Architecturerevived.blogspot.com, 4 May 2010. Web. 7 July 2012.

"Guangzhou Pearl River Tower by SOM." *Movingcities.org.* Movingcities.org, 2 Dec. 2009. Web. 17 Sept. 2012.

Hall, Peter. *Cities in Civilization.* N.p.: Fromm International, 2001. Print.

Hammond, Drew. "MAD UTOPIA : Look out World, Ma Yansong's Designs Envision a Bold Future." *Art and Living* Winter 2010: 115. Print.

"Hans Hollein; SBF Tower." *Designboom.com.* Designboom. com, n.d. Web. 18 Sept. 2012.

Hart, Sara. "Thermo-Bimetals in Action." *GreenSource Magazine* Jan.-Feb. 2013: 25. Print.

Hassan-Hardwick, Farrah. "Tall Buildings." *The Arup Journal* 2 (2012): 66. Print.

Hawthorne, Christopher. "Towering Symbolism Unchanged." *Los Angeles Times* 4 Sept. 2011: E6. Print.

Heap, Tom. "Masdar: Abu Dhabi's Carbon-Neutral City." *News. bbc.co.uk.* News.bbc.co.uk, 28 Mar. 2010. Web. 16 July 2012.

"Hegau Tower." *Aiachicago.org.* Aiachicago.org, n.d. Web. 17 Sept. 2012.

"Heliostats, Ho!" *Archidose.blogspot.com.* Archidose.blogspot. com, 8 Oct. 2010. Web. 27 Aug. 2012.

Herman, Kate. "Who's Tall Now?" *Architect* Apr. 2007: 38. Print.

Himelfarb, Ellen. "China Rising." *Azure Magazine* Sept. 2011: 86-87. Print.

Hughes, C. J. "Hudson Yards That Gleam in a Many Developer's Eye, Is At Last Going Up." *The New York Times* 21 Apr. 2013, Real Estate sec.: 10. Print.

Hughes, C. J. "Hudson Yards to Break Ground." *Architectural Record* Dec. 2012: 26. Print.

Hughes, C. J. "While Dubai Stumbles Abu Dhabi Matches On." *Architectural Record* May 2010: 30. Print.

"In Progress; Z Tower/ NRJA." *Archdoc.com.* Archdoc.com, n.d. Web. 28 Sept. 2012.

Iwamoto, Lisa. *Digital Fabrications: Architectural and Material Techniques.* Princeton: Princeton Architectural, 2009. Print

Jacobs, Karrie. "The Linear City." Dwell June 2010: 112. Print.

Jacobson, Clare. "A New Twist on Supertall." *Architectural Record* May 2012: 56-58. Print.

Jahn, Graham. "Piano in Sydney." *Architecturemedia.com.* Architecturemedia.com, Nov.-Dec. 2000. Web. 28 Aug. 2012.

Jodidio, Philip. *Architecture in the Emirates.* N.p.: Taschen, 2007. Print.

Jodidio, Philip. *Oscar Niemeyer.* N.p.: Taschen, 2013. Print.

"The John Hankock Center." *Chicagoarchitecture.info.* Chicagoarchitecture.info, 18 Sept. 2012. Web.

Johnson, Scott. *Tall Building: Imagining the Skyscraper.* Glendale, CA: Balcony Press, 2008. Print.

Kaijima, Moyomo, and Yoshiharu Tsukamoto. "Tokyo Flu, One City, Nine Flows." N.p., n.d. Web.

Kaijima, Moyomo. *Tokyo Flux, One City, Nine Flow Cities.* N.d. Essay. Tokyo, Japan.

Kang, Grace S., Alan Kren, and SEONCC Sustainable Design Committee Structural Sustainable Engineering Strategies Toward Sustainable Design. N.p.: n.p., n.d. Print.

Kassem, Fouad. "Changing the Shape of Abu Dhabi." *Urban Land* Spring 2009: 32-37. Print.

"KfW Westarkade Building Awarded Best Tall Building." *Domusweb.it.* Domusweb.it, 17 Nov. 2011. Web. 13 July 2012.

Kistler, William. "A Conversation with Lee Tabler." Urban Land Spring 2009: 38-42. Print.

Knecht, Barbara. "Commercial Buildings Open Their Windows." *Archrecord.construction.com.* Archrecord.construction.com, n.d. Web. 14 June 2012.

Knutt, Elaine. "Put It to the Panel." *Construction-manager.co.uk.* Construction-manager.co.uk, 18 Jan. 2010. Web. 27 Aug. 2012.

Koolhaas, Rem. *Project Japan: Metabolism Talks.* N.p.: Taschen, 2011. Print.

"KPF's Pinnacle in Danger of Demolition." *Ctbuh.org.* N.p., 4 Feb. 2013. Web. 14 May 2013.

Kumpusch, Christoph A. *The Light Pavilion by Lebbeus Woods and Christoph A. Kumpusch for the Sliced Porosity Block in Chengdu, China, 2007-2012.* N.p.: Lars Muller, 2013. Print.

Lee, Evelyn. "New Green Building in Miami :The COR Building." *Inhabitat.com.* Inhabitat.com, 12 Nov. 2006. Web. 12 Nov. 2006.

Lentz, Linda. "Asymptote Illuminates the Fast Track." *Architectural Record* May 2010: 102-03. Print.

Leslie, Thomas. "Heights of Fancy." *The New York Times* 31 May 2013: A19. Print.

"The Life and Death of a Great American City 2001 - 2011." *Architectural Record* Sept. 2011: 53-78. Print.

Linn, Charles. "Case Study: Manitoba Hydro Place." *Greensourceconstruction.com.* Greensourceconstruction. com, n.d. Web. 14 June 2012.

Linn, Charles. "Case Study; Manitoba Hydro Place." *Greensource.construction.com.* Greensource.construction.com, n.d. Web. 14 June 2012.

Lubell, Sam. "It's Not Just The Gargoyles Anymore." *The New York Times* 31 Mar. 2013: 8. Print.

Lubell, Sam. "Paris Gives Itself a Futuristic Transplant." *Nytimes.com.* Nytimes.com, 6 May 2007. Web.

M, J. "Cultured Pearl: Working in Hot House of China, SOM Attempt to Radically Redefine the Relationship between Tall Buildings and Their Energy Consumption." *The Architectural Review* Oct. 2008: 66-67. Print.

M, J. "Cultured Pearl: Working in Hot House of China, SOM Attempt to Radically Redefine the Relationship between Tall Buildings and Their Energy Consumption." *The Architectural Review* Oct. 2008: 66-67. Print.

"MAD Architects / Ma Yansong." *Designboom.com.* Designboom.com, n.d. Web. 17 Sept. 2012.

Malin, Nadav. "Case Studies Climate Connections." *Greensourcemag.com* Jan.-Feb. 2013: 43-49. Print.

Mandelbrot, Benoit. *The Fractal Geometry of Nature.* N.p.: W.H. Freeman and Company, 1982. Print

Schiler, Marc. "Performative Facades: A Proposed Definition." *Facade Tectonics.* Proc. of Facade Tectonics: The Building Envelope 13, School of Architecture University of Southern California, Los Angeles. Vol. 13. N.p.: n.p., n.d. 13. Print.

Mara, Felix. "KfW Westarkade Offices and Conference Centre Frankfurt, by Sauerbruch Hutton." *Architectsjournal.co.uk.* Architectsjournal.co.uk, 10 Mar. 2011. Web. 13 July 2012.

Magnier, Mark. "There's No Place Like Home: At the Top of India's Growing List of Billionaires, Mukesh Ambani Has a House Boasting 27 Floors, Ocean and Slum Views." *Los Angeles Times* 25 Oct. 2010: A10+. Print.

Mathews, Neelam, and James Murdock. "Perkins + Will Debunks Antilla Myths." *Archrecord.construction.com.* Archrecord.construction.com, 18 Oct. 2007. Web. 14 Sept. 2012.

Mayne, Thom. *Combinatory Urbanism: The Complex Behavior of Collective Form.* N.p.: Stray Dog Cafe, 2011. Print.

Mazzoleni, Ilaria. *Architecture Follows Nature-Biomimetic Principles for Innovative Design.* N.p.: CRC, 2013. Print.

McKechnie, Steve. "The Pinnacle." *The Arup Journal* 2 (2012): 77-84. Print.

Mertins, Detlef, and Patrik Schumacher. *Zaha Hadid.* N.p.: Guggenheim Museum, 2006. Print.

Meyer, Ulf. "Case Study: KfW Westarkade." *Greensourceconstruction.com.* Greensourceconstruction.com, May 2011. Web. 14 June 2012.

Meyer, Ulf. "Case Study: KfW Westarkade." *Greensource.construction.com.* Greensource.construction.com, May 2011. Web. 14 June 2012.

Michler, Andrew. "Korean Tower Boasts One of World's Most Efficient Solar Facades." *Inhabitant.com.* Inhabitant.com, 29 Oct. 2010. Web.

Minutillo, Josephine. "Hans Hollein Tried Something New by Doing Something Old." *Architectural Record* Aug. 2010: 35. Print.

Minutillo, Josephine. "Tall Buildings Push Limits by Stepping Up, Not Back." *Architectural Record* Apr. 2009: 117-22. Print.

Mori Building Co., Ltd. *Roppongi Hills Opening Exhibition: The Global City.* N.p.: n.p., n.d. Print.

Mostafavi, Mohsen, and Gareth Doherty. *Ecological Urbanism.* N.p.: Lars Muller, 2010. Print.

Moza, Ezra A. From *"Advertising Architecture"* to *"Media Facade": Communication through Digital Display Skin.* Thesis. Epoka University, n.d. N.p.: n.p., 2012. Print.

Munro, Dominic, Mark Richards, and Andrew Smith. "Heron Tower." *The Arup Journal* 2 (2012): 85-92. Print.

"MVRDV and ADEPT Architects 'Sky Village' Wins Copenhagen Competition." *Designboom.com.* Designboom.com, n.d. Web. 28 Sept. 2012.

Nadal, Luc. "City Center Revitalization: Tapping São Paulo's Global Potential." *Sustainable Transport* 18 (2006): 16-20. Print.

Nayeri, Farah. "Shard Architect Renzo Piano Says Tower Not Arrogant." *Businessweek.com.* Businessweek.com, 04 July 2012. Web.

"New Facade for Port Authority." *Timesquare.com.* Timesquare.com, 10 May 2011. Web.

"NHN : Green Factory." *Designboom.com.* Designboom.com, n.d. Web. 28 Aug. 2012.

Nobel, Philip. "Close Reading: Frank Lloyd Wright's Mile-High." *Nytimes.com.* Nytimes.com, 17 Oct. 2004. Web.

"Northern Star : At the Northern Limit for Tall Buildings, Foster's Daring Russia Tower Tests Extremes of Scale, Structure and Form." *Architectural Record* Oct. 2008: 46-49. Print.

Nozawa, Dr., Yasushi. "The Direction of Urban Regeneration in Tokyo." CITY FUTURES; An International Conference on Globalism and Urban Change. Chicago. Sept. 2012. Lecture.

O'Hagan, Simon. "Renzo Piano: "The Shard Is My Dream"" *Independent.co.uk.* Independent.co.uk, 8 Apr. 2012. Web.

Oldfield, Philip. "The Tallest 20 in 2020." *The Big Project* Feb. 2008: 36. Print.

"On Parametric Typology." *Pliplicplex.blogspot.com.* Pliplicplex.blogspot.com, 14 Nov. 2011. Web. 12 June 2012.

"Oscar! 1907 - 2012." *Wallpaper* Feb. 2013: 003. Print.

Ouroussoff, Nicolai. "Downtown Skyscraper For The Digital Age." *The New York Times* 10 Feb. 2011, The Arts sec.: 8. Print.

Ouroussoff, Nicolai. "Near-Empty Tower Still Holds Hope." *The New York Times* 29 June 2010, The Arts sec.: 6. Print.

Ouroussoff, Nicolai. "Off With Its Top! City Cuts Tower to Size." *The New York Times* 9 Sept. 2009: 6. Print.

Ouroussoff, Nicolai. "Remaking Paris." *Nytimes.com.* Nytimes.com, 8 June 2009. Web.

Page, Andrew. "Australia's Greenest Skyscraper Has a Highly Energy-Efficient Glass Skin." *Glassquarterly.com.* Glassquarterly.com, 18 Feb. 2012. Web. 17 Sept. 2012.

"Parametric Consultation New York Tower Proposal." *Livearchitecturenetwork.net.* Livearchitecturenetwork.net, July 2009. Web. 28 Sept. 2012.

Pasternack, Alex. "How Green Buildings Should Look: Ken Yeang." *Treehugger.com.* Treehugger.com, 19 Mar. 2009. Web.

Pauwels, Martine. "Paris Business Hub Goes on Defense." *The Wall Street Journal* [New York] 2 May 2012, Money & Investing sec.: C1. Print.

Pearson, Clifford A. "Case Study: Vanke Center." *Greensourceconstruction.com.* Greensourceconstruction.com, Mar. 2011. Web. June 2012.

Peer, Basharat. "Modern Mecca : The Transformation of a Holy

City." *The New Yorker* 16 Apr. 2012: 75-81. Print.

"Perkins + Will Takes out a Future Projects Award for Al Birr Project." *Bustler*. Buster, 11 Feb. 2010. Web. 28 Aug. 2012.

Perlman, Janice. *Favela: Four Decades of Living on the Edge in Rio De Janeiro*. N.p.: Oxford UP, USA, 2011. Print.

Perlman, Janice. *Sharing Approaches That Work: Transfer and Adaptation of Urban Innovations*. Rep. N.p.: Mega Cities Project, n.d. Print.

Pilling, David. "The Rise of The Megacity." *The Financial Times*. Slate.com, 5 Nov. 2011. Web. 17 Sept. 2012.

Pollock, Naomi R. "A Shut and Open Case : Shigeru Ban Transports His Unique Japanese Sensibilities to a Chelsea Condominium with High Line Views." *Architectural Record* Sept. 2011: 90-92. Print.

Poucke, Van. "Arab World Institute by Jean Nouvel." *Kineticarchitecture.net*. Kineticarchitecture.net, 31 Jan. 2011. Web. 8 Aug. 2012.

Richie, Donald. *Tokyo Megacity*. N.p.: Tuttle, 2010. Print.

Risbud, Aditi. "Berkeley Lab Researchers Develop New Infrared Coating for Windows." *Newscenter.lbl.gov*. Newscenter.lbl.gov, 06 Sept. 2011. Web.

Romero, Simon. "The New New São Paulo." *The New York Times Magazine* Mar. 2013: 117+. Print.

Ross, Philip. "Typology Quaterly." *The Architectural Review* Aug. 2012: 75-85. Print.

Saber, Khalifa. "11 Super-Green Skyscrapers." *Altdotenergy.com*. Altdotenergy.com, 23 Oct. 2008. Web. 15 June 2012.

Saich, Nico. "Museum Plaza / REX." *Archdaily.com*. Archdaily.com, 10 Feb. 2009. Web.

"São Paulo." *Wikipedia.com*. Wikipedia.com, n.d. Web. 25 Nov. 2012.

Sarkisian, Mark, Keith Boswell, Neville Mathias, and Eric Long. *Jinao Tower: The Design Integration of Structural Efficiency, Architectural Expression and High Performance Exterior Wall Systems*. Tech. N.p.: n.p., n.d. Print.

Sassen, Saskia. *The Global City*. N.p.: Princeton UP, 2001. Print.

"SBF Tower / Atelier Hollein." Archdaily.com. Archdaily.com, n.d. Web. 18 Sept. 2012.

Schiler, Marc. "Performative Facades: A Proposed Definition." *Facade Tectonics*. Proc. of Facade Tectonics: The Building Envelope 13, School of Architecture University of Southern California, Los Angeles. Vol. 13. N.p.: n.p., n.d. 13. Print

Schmidt, John R. "Frank Lloyd Wright's Mile-High Building." *Wbez.org*. Wbez.org, 25 Aug. 2011. Web.

Schumacher, Patrik. "Parametricism as Style: Parametricist Manifesto." *Patrikschumacher.com*. Patrickschumacher.com, 2008. Web. 11 May 2012.

Schumacher Patrik, *The Autopoiesis of Architecture*, London : John Wiley & Sons Ltd, 2010. Print

Shane, David G. *Urban Design Since 1945: A Global Perspective*. Chichester, West Sussex: John Wiley & Sons, 2011. Print.

Sharpley, Richard. *The Challenges of Economic Diversification Through Tourism: The Case for Abu Dhabi*. N.p.: Wiley Interscience, 2002. Print.

Shockley, Jennifer. "Bahrain World Trade Center By Atkins." *Greenbuildingelements.com*. Greenbuildingelements.com, 28 Sept. 2011. Web. 18 June 2012.

Slackman, Michael. "Piercing the Sky Amid a Deflating Economy." *The New York Times* 14 Jan. 2010: A10. Print.

Snoonian, Deborah. "SOM Aims to Build a Zero-Energy Office Tower in Guangdong." *Archrecord.construction.com*. Archrecord.construction.com, 4 Apr. 2006. Web.

Sorensen, Andre. *Building World City Tokyo: Globalization and Conflict Over Urban Space*. N.p.: Annals of Regional Science, n.d. Print.

"Spacelab Cook-Fournier Kunsthaus Graz." *Arcspace.com*. Arcspace.com, n.d. Web. 28 Sept. 2012.

Sparks, Ian. "Toppled by the French! London's Shard Will Soon Loose Title of Europe' S Tallest Building to Hermitage Plaza in Paris." *Dailymail.co.uk*. Dailymail.co.uk, 9 Mar. 2012. Web.

Stephens, Suzanne. "0- 14 Tower Reiser + Umemoto." *Archrecord.construction.com*. Archrecord.construction.com, n.d. Web. 17 Oct. 2012.

Stephens, Suzanne. "Enter the Dragon." *Architectural Record* May 2012: 143-47. Print.

Stephens, Suzanne, Ian Luna, and Ron Broadhurst. *Imagining Ground Zero: The Official and Unofficial Proposals for the World Trade Center Site*. N.p.: Rizzoli, 2004. Print.

"Steven Holl Architects to Build Porosity Block in Chengdu, China." *Steveholl.com*. Stevenholl.com, n.d. Web. 27 Aug. 2012.

"Steven Holl's Porosity Block Tops Out." *Architizer.com*. Architzer.com, 6 Sept. 2011. Web.

Studioplex Volume 1: Architecture, a Timely Matter. N.p.: Takashi Kishi/ SOGO SHIKAKU, 2012. Print.

Such, Robert. "WOHA and RealU Craft a Crystalline Hybrid." *Architectural Record* May 2010: 98-100. Print.

Thompson, D'Arcy W. *On Growth and Form*. 1st ed. N.p.: n.p., 1917. Print.

Tohill, Joseph. "Construction Begins for Plantagon Vertical Farm in Sweden." *The9billion.com*. The9billion.com, 22 Feb. 2012. Web. 27 Aug. 2012.

Tojner, Poul E., Ole Thyssen, Kasper Guldager, and Wilfried Wang. *Green Architecture for the Future*. N.p.: Louisiana Museum of Modern Art, 2010. Print.

"Tree Trunk Towers: Cantilevered Floor / Super Core Structure." Architect Aug. 2011: 112. Print.

van Berkel, Ben. "Interviews: Raffles City Hangzhou." *Http://www.unstudio.com*. N.p., n.d. Web.

Venturi, Robert, Denise Scott Brown, and Steven Izenour. *Learning from Las Vegas*. Cambridge, MA: MIT, 1972. Print.

Vivian, Philip. "1 Bligh Street." *Australiandesignreview.com*. Australiandesignreview.com, 1 Mar. 2012. Web. 27 May 2012.

Vollers, Dr Karel. "Free - D High Rises." *Structuremag.org*. Structuremag.org, June 2008. Web.

Weinstock, Michael. "Self Organization and Material Constructions." *Architectural Design* Mar.-Apr. 2006: 34-41. Print.

Williams, Austin. "Chinese Chequers; The "Sliced Porosity" of Steven Holl's Latest Chinese Mega Project Is a Graphic Presence Implanted in the Pulsating Heart of Chengdu." *The Architectural Review* Mar. 2013: n. pag. Web.

Williams, Timothy. "Here Comes the Sun, Redirected." *Nytimes.com*. Nytimes.com, 2 June 2005. Web.

Wing, Jimmie. "Star Place, Kaohsiung, Taiwan." *Mondoarc.com*.

Mondoarc.com, Apr.-May 2009. Web.

Woodfield, Peter. "London Towers Rising on Mideast Money." *The Global Edition of the New York Times* 6 Aug. 2009: 15. Print.

"The World's First Plantagon Greenhouse for Urban Agriculture Breaks Ground in Sweden." *Designitgreener.com*. Designitgreener.com, n.d. Web.

"Xicui Entertainment Complex Beijing, China." *The Architects Newspaper* 17 Sept. 2008: 19. Print.

Yardley, Jim. "Soaring Above India's Poverty, a 27-Story Home." *Nytimes.com*. Nytimes.com, 28 Oct. 2010. Web.

Yeang, Ken. *Eco Skyscrapers*. Vol. 2. N.p.: Mages Dist Ac, 2011. Print.

"You'll Be Blown Away: BFLS Completes Strata SE1 First Building in the World with Integral Wind Turbines." *Worldarchitecturenews.com*. Worldarchitecturenews.com, 03 Aug. 2010. Web. 7 July 2012.

Yudelson, Jerry. "Water Use and Green Building." *Greenbuildingpro.com*. Greenbuildingpro.com, 17 Sept. 2010. Web. 18 Sept. 2012.

Zaera-Polo, Alejandro. "A Taxonomy of Towers." *Harvard Design Magazine* 26 (2007): n. pag. Print.

PHOTOGRAPHY CREDITS

End Pages
8 Spruce, Courtesy of Gehry Partners
30
National Library of France © Georges Fessy / DPA / Adagp
Arab World Institute © Philippe Ruault
31
Kempinski Hotel and Residences SailTower, Courtesy of Perkins + Will
GSW Headquarters, Jan Bitter
32
Next Human Network (NHN) Headquarters © Park Young Chae Photography
33
Caltrans District 7 Headquarters, Used with Permission, Stephen Friday
41 Cooper Square, Used with Permission, Beyond My Ken
34
Hegau Tower © Rainer Viertlboeck
35
Metal Shutter Houses, Courtesy of Shigeru Ban Architects
Media-TIC, Courtesy of Javier Gutiérrez Marcos
36,37
Al Bahr ADIC Towers © Aedas
38,39
Bloom, Materials & Applications Exhibit, Courtesy of DO|SU Studio Architecture
40
1 Bligh Office Tower © H.G. Esch
41
RWE Headquarters © H.G. Esch
42
Manitoba Hydro © Maris Mezulis
43
Macquarie Apartments Aurora Place, Courtesy of Renzo Piano Building Workshop
44
Shanghai Tower Skygarden Section, Courtesy of Gensler
45
Al-Birr Foundation Headquarters, Perkins + Will
46
Heron Tower, Used with Permission Eluveitie
47
Federation of Korean Industries Tower, Courtesy of AS+GG
49
The Cooperative Insurance Society (CIS), Courtsey of Steve Thornton
50
30 St Mary Axe "Gherkin", Copyright Foster and Partners
KfW Westarkade, Courtesy of Ken Lee
51
Strata SE1, Duncan Wren
Bahrain World Trade Center, Courtesy of Atkins

52
COR Tower Miami, Courtesy of Oppenheim Architecture+Design
Pearl River Tower, Used with Permission IndexxRus
53
Wuhan Greenland Center, Courtesy of AS+GG
55
EDITT Tower © T.R.Hamzah Yeang Sdn. Bhd. (Malaysia)
Planted Tower of Nantes, Courtesy of Maison Édouard François
Menara Mesiniaga © T.R.Hamzah Yeang Sdn. Bhd. (Malaysia)
56
SIEEB Sino- Italian and Energy Efficient Building, Courtesy of Luning Li
60
Crystal Palace, Used with Permission Tldtld
Glass Skyscraper, Digital Image © The Museum of Modern Art/ Licensed by SCALA / Art Resource, NY; © 2008 Artists Rights Society (ARS), New York / VG Bild-Kunst, Bonn
Bauhaus Building, Dessau, Lincensed by Art Resource / Artists Rights Society (ARS), New York
65
Willis Faber & Dumas Office © Ken Kirkwood
Apple Store Fifth Avenue, Used with Permission Fletcher6 / © 2013 Artists Rights Society (ARS), New York / VG Bild-Kunst, Bonn
67
Corrugated Glass _Casa De Musica, Christian Richters Photography
Fritted Glass, Tekena koko
Films and Vinyl, Tekena koko
68,69
Louvres, Melbourne Elm Apartments, Courtesy of Peter Clarke Photography
69
Fabric (silicone)_ UBPA B3-2 Pavilion, Courtesy of Studio Archea / Luciano Romano
70
Metal Meshes, Caltrans District 7 Headquarters, Courtesy of Ximo Michavila
Bent glass, IAC Building, By permission Courtesy of Xaal
73
Kunsthaus, By Permission Stephan Weinberger
74
Maison de la publicite, Licensed by Art Resource / Artists Rights Society (ARS), New York
75
Times Square, New York City, By Permission Terabass
Las Vegas Strip, By Permission Clément Bardot
77
Iluma, Courtesy of WOHA/Patrick Bingham-Hall

78
Star Place © UNStudio / Christian Ritchers
79
The Port Authority Bus Terminal, Courtesy of A2a Media
Yas Hotel, Courtesy of Gary McGovern
Galleria Center City © UNStudio / Kim Yong- Kwan
85
D'Arcy Wentworth Thompson, By Permission Shyamal
87
Mandelbrot Set, By Permission Wolfgang Beyer
Embryological House, Courtesy of Greg Lynn Form
88, 89
Huaxi Urban Centre Tower, Courtesy of Tom Wiscombe Design
91
Aeon II, Courtesy of Reiser + Umemoto, RUR Architecture P.C
Absolute Towers, Courtesy of MAD Architects / Tom Arban
92, 93, 95
Raffles City © UNStudio
97, 98
Phare Tower, Courtesy Morphosis
100
8 Spruce Street, By Permission Jim Henderson; Courtesy Gehry Partners
101
8 Spruce, Photo © dbox
102
8 Spruce Street, By Permission Jim Henderson; Courtesy Gehry Partners
106
One-Mile-High Skyscraper © The Frank Lloyd Wright Foundation, AZ; Artists Rights Society (ARS), NY
Downtown Athletic Club, Duncan Hunter
107
John Hancock Center, By Permission Joe Ravi
108
Shanghai Tower, Courtsey of Gensler
109
Shard, Courtesy of Renzo Piano Building Workshop
110, 111
Russia Tower © Foster + Partners
112
Parallax Towers, Couretesty of Steven Holl Architects
Simmons Hall MIT, By Permission Mido
113
Linked Hybrid © Shu He
CCTV Headquarters, axonometric view of the building, Office for Metropolitan Architecture (OMA)
Vanke Center, Shenzhen © Iwan Baan
116, 117
Sliced Porosity Block - CapitaLand Raffles City Chengdu © Shu He; Courtesy of Steven Holl Architects
117
Matrix Gateway Complex, Courtesy of AS+GG
118
Sky Village © ADEPT ApS
119
56 Leonard Street © Herzog & de Meuron
120
Commerzbank Headquarters © Foster + Partners
Yongsan International Business District "Project R6" © REX

121
Yongsan International Business District Cross # Towers © BIG, *8 House* © BIG
123
West 57 © BIG
Beach and Howe © BIG / Luxigon
Marina Bay Sands Resort, By Permission Someformofhuman
124
Vertical Neighborhood, MoMA Tower, Courtesy Axis Mund
Antilia Towers © ER
130, 131
Manhattan Aerial View Looking North, By Permission Tm Wikipedia Commons
134, 135
London Skyline, By Permission David Iliff
138, 139
Paris Skyline, La Defense, Courtesy of Presanna Kumar
142, 143
Tokyo Skyline Wikipedia Commons
146, 147
Shanghai Skyline, By Permission Peter Shamray
150, 151
Abu Dhabi Skyline, Beno Saradzic
154, 155
São Paulo Skyline, By Permission Francisco Anzola

ACKNOWLEDGEMENTS

I would like to thank the many established architects with whom I have had the pleasure to work. To Sally Harkness of The Architects' Collaborative in Cambridge, Massachusetts for her knowledge of programming and the illumination of tall buildings. To Chuck Bassett of the San Francisco office of Skidmore, Owings & Merrill for his experience in the design of tall office buildings. To Philip Johnson and John Burgee for their attention to cultural history and its bearing on architectural form and detail. To William L. Pereira for his imaginative futurism and the confidence to provide us a platform to pursue our own ideas at Johnson Fain.

In academia, I remain indebted to Ray Kappe, an esteemed architect and the founder and former Director at SCI-Arc for a first teaching post and to Richard Weinstein, Dean Emeritus at UCLA's School of Architecture & Urban Planning for the opportunity to teach graduate students about the diversity of tall buildings in Los Angeles. I have benefited from my association with Qingyun Ma, Dean and Della & Harry MacDonald Chair at USC's School of Architecture for faculty participation at the School and Jennifer Wolch, William W. Wurster Dean of the College of Environmental Design at the University of California, Berkeley for her pursuit of sustainable architectures.

In the endeavor of designing and constructing tall buildings, I wish to thank our many exceptional clients in the US and abroad who are too numerous to mention. Collaborating with us, we have learned much from Bruce McKinley, Matt Williams and Russell Fortmeyer of the Los Angeles office of ARUP and Dr. Anders Carlson of Simpson Gumpertz & Heger. In Dallas, we've been fortunate to work with the late Dr. Cyrus Cantrell III, a physicist, engineer and computer science pioneer and in New York, Gordon Smith, the pre-eminent glazing and curtain wall consultant.

I wish to thank the principals and design staff at Johnson Fain. Thanks go to our advanced modeling staff for their support and review of the Performative Parametrics essay: Jed Donaldson, Nick Martinez, Layton Petersen and Ben Tamuno-koko. Thanks also to Ben for pictorial research, editing and text support, to principal Mark Gershen and to Natalie Egnatchik, my assistant. Thanks always to Bill Fain, my invaluable partner at Johnson Fain.

A note of special appreciation goes to Carol Willis, director of The Skyscraper Museum in New York City for good counsel and for single-handedly keeping all eyes on the topic. A special thanks to Joseph Giovannini who has expanded the realm of this book with his insightful preface. Thanks to Frank Gehry, Craig Webb and John Bowers for availing us of the graphic for the book's end pages. Finally, thanks to Ann Gray, publisher and editor at Balcony Media, her staff and Jean-Marc Durviaux at Distinc for this, our third project together. Thanks to all.